Study Guide

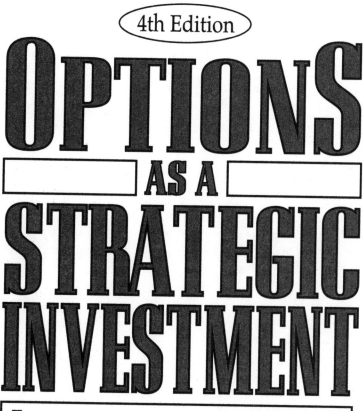

4th Edition

OPTIONS
AS A
STRATEGIC
INVESTMENT

Lawrence G. McMillan

NYIF

NEW YORK INSTITUTE OF FINANCE

NEW YORK • TORONTO • SYDNEY • TOKYO • SINGAPORE

NEW YORK INSTITUTE OF FINANCE
NYIF and NEW YORK INSTITUTE OF FINANCE are trademarks of
Executive Tax Reports, Inc. used under license by Penguin Putnam Inc.

Printed in the United States of America
10 9 8 7 6 5 4 3 2

ISBN 0-7352-0238-9

Contents

How to Use
This Study Guide

This study guide has been prepared by the New York Institute of Finance with the cooperation and input of Lawrence G. McMillan.

The guide is designed to be used exclusively with the first 25 chapters of Lawrence G. McMillan's *Options as a Strategic Investment*, fourth edition (referred to as the "text").

The guide's objective is to test—and thereby to ensure—your comprehension of the large body of knowledge associated with option strategies explained in the first 25 chapters of the text.

The methodology is simple to follow and uses your time efficiently. Here are the recommended steps:

- Before reading the text, go to Lesson 1 in the *Study Guide* (page 1). There you will find a Reading Assignment, which for the first lesson is Chapter 1 of the text. You will also find one or more Objectives and a list of Key Terms. Following each term is a page reference indicating where in the text you can find a definition or explanation of the term. Pay special attention to these terms.

- Read the chapter assigned for the lesson. As you read, stay aware of the objectives and key terms. Ask questions of the text. Don't be afraid to underline what you feel is important—or make marginal notes.

- Go to the Challenge section of the lesson. Answer the questions there as best you can "closed book."

- Then go to the Answer Sheet and compare your answers with those given. If necessary, go to the places in the text that explain the answers (page references are given).

- To grade yourself, divide your correct answers by the total number of questions, and multiply the result by 100. This is your percentage correct. If the percentage is less than 65%, you should re-read the material for that lesson.

The purpose of this comparison, however, is not to give yourself a grade. Rather, it is to determine the areas where your comprehension is weak. Toward that end, each answer has a page reference to the text and a brief explanation of why the answer is correct. We suggest that you follow up these page references by re-reading the relevant sections of the text and making sure you understand the answer.

This guide has been produced with the utmost concern for accuracy and freedom from error. However, we welcome your comments with regard to improvement.

New York Institute of Finance

Definitions

READING ASSIGNMENT

Chapter 1 of the text.

OBJECTIVE

By the end of this lesson, you should be able to:
   Explain the basic terms associated with option strategies.

KEY TERMS

   assignment, 6
   automatic exercise, 18
   call option, 3
   call option price curve, 10
   Chicago Board Options Exchange (CBOE), 22
   class, 5
   closing transaction, 6
   derivative security, 4
   early exercise, 19
   exercise price, 3
   good-until-canceled order, 34
   holder, 6
   in-the-money, 7
   intrinsic value, 7
   LEAPS option, 26
   limit order, 33
   margin, 16

CHALLENGE

MATCHING QUIZ

Match each term in the left column with a definition from the right column, by placing the number of the definition in the space next to the term.

_____	**A.** assignment	**1.** The right to sell an underlying security at a certain price for a certain amount of time.
_____	**B.** call option	**2.** Option seller.
_____	**C.** derivative security	**3.** A code used to designate the terms of an option contract.
_____	**D.** exercise price	**4.** All contracts of the same class having the same expiration date and striking price.
_____	**E.** good-until-canceled order	**5.** Relationship that occurs when the underlying security is trading at its intrinsic value.

_____	**F.** holder	**6.** An initial buy or sell.
_____	**G.** intrinsic value	**7.** An order that becomes a limit order when the specified price is reached.
_____	**H.** LEAPS option	**8.** The price at which the stock underlying an option may be bought or sold.
_____	**I.** margin	**9.** The amount by which the option premium exceeds the intrinsic value.
_____	**J.** market not held order	**10.** The amount by which the stock price exceeds the striking price.
_____	**K.** open interest	**11.** The stock on which an option contract is based.
_____	**L.** opening transaction	**12.** An order that gives the floor broker discretion in executing the order.
_____	**M.** parity	**13.** The right to buy an underlying security at a certain price for a certain amount of time.
_____	**N.** put option	**14.** An order that remains valid for 6 months if not renewed by the customer.
_____	**O.** series	**15.** The total number of all opening and closing transactions still outstanding.
_____	**P.** stop-limit order	**16.** Collateral necessary for the purchase of stock or the financing of option transactions.
_____	**Q.** symbol	**17.** The carrying out of the obligation of the writer to fulfill the terms of an option contract.
_____	**R.** time value premium	**18.** Option owner or buyer.
_____	**S.** underlying security	**19.** An option that will expire in one or more years.
_____	**T.** writer	**20.** A security that is irrevocably linked to its underlying stock.

FILL-INS

Fill in the blanks with the correct words or phrases.

1. A transaction that reduces an investor's position in an option is called a
   _____.

2. A call option is _____ if the stock is selling below the
   striking price of the option.

3. The call option price curve plots the price of an option against
   _____.

4. Figure 1-2 shows that the time value premium is greatest when
   _____.

5. The risk-free interest rate is generally the current rate of
   _____.

6. The OCC automatically exercises a call that is _____ in-
   the-money at expiration.

7. Market-makers are assigned to make markets on optionable stocks by the
   _____.

8. Option trades have a _____ settlement cycle.

9. For purposes of determining position limits, long calls and
   _____ are on the same side of the market.

10. A good-till-canceled order remains valid for _____ unless
    extended by the investor.

MULTIPLE CHOICE

Circle the letter of the correct answer.

1. The four specifications that describe an option contract are:
   a. type, expiration date, ex-dividend date, and striking price
   b. type, underlying stock, ex-dividend date, and striking price
   c. type, underlying stock, expiration date, and striking price
   d. underlying stock, expiration date, ex-dividend date, and striking price

2. The terms of a listed option are affected by:
   a. splits only
   b. splits and cash dividends
   c. splits, stock dividends, and cash dividends
   d. splits and stock dividends

3. The last trading day for an option is:
   a. the first Friday of the expiration month
   b. the third Friday of the expiration month
   c. the last Friday of the expiration month
   d. the third Saturday of the expiration month

4. A call option is in-the-money if:
   a. The stock price is above the striking price of the option.
   b. The stock price is below the striking price of the option.
   c. The stock price is the same as the striking price of the option.
   d. The stock price is rising.

5. The four major determinants of an option's price are:
   a. price of the underlying, striking price, time remaining, and risk-free interest rate
   b. striking price, time remaining, volatility, and risk-free interest rate
   c. price of the underlying, striking price, time remaining, and volatility
   d. price of the underlying, striking price, time remaining, and dividend rate

6. The expiration month code for a call option expiring in August is:
   a. H
   b. V
   c. E
   d. T

7. The expiration month code for a put option expiring in March is:
   a. Y
   b. C
   c. F
   d. O

8. The striking price code for a call priced at 315.00 is:
   a. A
   b. C
   c. Q
   d. T

9. The striking price code for a put priced at 47.50 is usually:
   a. I
   b. V
   c. M
   d. W

10. Which of these types of orders is (are) acceptable on all option exchanges?
    a. Limit orders
    b. Market not held orders
    c. Market orders
    d. All of the above

ANSWER SHEET

MATCHING QUIZ

A. 17	**K.** 15
B. 13	**L.** 6
C. 20	**M.** 5
D. 8	**N.** 1
E. 14	**O.** 4
F. 18	**P.** 7
G. 10	**Q.** 3
H. 19	**R.** 9
I. 16	**S.** 11
J. 12	**T.** 2

FILL-INS

1. A transaction that reduces an investor's position in an option is called a <u>closing transaction</u>. (Page 6)

2. A call option is <u>out-of-the-money</u> if the stock is selling below the striking price of the option. (Page 7)

3. The call option price curve plots the price of an option against <u>the price of its underlying security</u>. (Page 10)

4. Figure 1-2 shows that the time value premium is greatest when <u>the stock price and the striking price are the same</u>. (Page 11)

5. The risk-free interest rate is generally the current rate of <u>90-day Treasury bills</u>. (Page 14)

6. The OCC automatically exercises a call that is <u>75 cents</u> in-the-money at expiration. (Page 18)

7. Market-makers are assigned to make markets on optionable stocks by the <u>CBOE</u>. (Page 22)

8. Option trades have a <u>one-day</u> settlement cycle. (Page 28)

9. For purposes of determining position limits, long calls and <u>short puts</u> are on the same side of the market. (Page 31)

10. A good-till-canceled order remains valid for <u>6 months</u> unless extended by the investor. (Page 34)

MULTIPLE CHOICE

1. **c** See page 4 of the text.

2. **d** See page 4 of the text.

3. **b** See page 5 of the text. Even though an option technically expires on a Saturday, an investor who wishes to exercise an option must notify a broker of that intention by 5:30 P.M. (EST) on Friday

4. **a** See page 7 of the text. Note that put options work in a converse manner.

5. **c** See page 9 of the text. The risk-free interest rate and the dividend rate are generally less important factors.

6. **a** See page 23 of the text.

7. **d** See page 23 of the text.

8. **b** See page 24 of the text.

9. **d** See page 25 of the text.

10. **d** See pages 32–33 of the text. Because regulations change, an investor should always confirm with a broker that an order is valid for a given exchange.

Covered Call Writing

READING ASSIGNMENT

Chapter 2 of the text.

OBJECTIVES

By the end of this lesson, you should be able to:

Compute a return on investment.

Execute a covered write order correctly.

Select the appropriate covered write.

KEY TERMS

CHALLENGE

MATCHING QUIZ

Match each term in the left column with a definition from the right column, by placing the number of the definition in the space next to the term.

_____ **A.** conservative covered call write

1. The return an investor realizes if the underlying stock is called away.

_____ **B.** downside break-even point

2. The cost of a covered writing position, subtracting the call price from the stock price.

_____ **C.** incremental return concept

3. Buying back a call when the stock price drops and then selling a call with a lower striking price.

_____ **D.** net price

4. Stock price minus call price.

_____ **E.** return if exercised

5. Strategy of writing calls near the striking price to achieve the best balance between maximum potential return and downside protection.

_____ **F.** return if unchanged

6. Buying back a call when the stock price rises and then selling a call with a higher striking price.

_____ **G.** rolling down

7. The return an investor realizes if the underlying stock is unchanged at expiration.

_____ **H.** rolling forward

8. Buying back a call and selling a longer-term call with the same striking price.

_____	**I.** rolling up	**9.** Selling a call option while simultaneously owning the obligated number of shares of the underlying stock.
_____	**J.** total return concept	**10.** Strategy of rolling up for credits to a predetermined target price and then allowing the stock to be called away.

FILL-INS

Fill in the blanks with the correct words or phrases.

1. The primary objective of covered writing is _____.

2. An investment position that offers less risk generally has _____.

3. The return if unchanged is also called the _____.

4. When commissions are taken into account, the more shares an investor writes against, the _____ the returns and the _____ the break-even point will be.

5. Writing half of the position against in-the-moneys and half against out-of-the-moneys on the same stock is called a _____.

6. Rolling down generally reduces the _____ of a position.

7. Simultaneously buying one call and selling another results in a _____ position.

8. When an investor _____, a debit is incurred.

9. A convertible security that has been called by the company trades at the _____.

10. The key to successfully implementing the incremental return strategy is to _____.

MULTIPLE CHOICE

Circle the letter of the correct answer.

1. A covered call write generates a loss when:
   a. The stock rises by a distance greater than the call option premium.
   b. The stock falls by a distance greater than the call option premium.
   c. The option expires at parity.
   d. The option is called away.

2. The downside break-even point for a covered write is:
   a. stock price minus call price
   b. stock price plus call price
   c. strike price minus call price
   d. strike price minus stock price

3. The strategy of owning the stock and writing the call will outperform stock ownership in which of the following cases?
   a. The stock price falls.
   b. The stock price remains the same.
   c. The stock price rises slightly.
   d. All of the above.

4. The total return concept of covered writing involves all of the following **EXCEPT**:
   a. achieving downside protection
   b. achieving maximum potential return
   c. retaining stock ownership
   d. allowing stock to be called away

5. Before taking a position, an investor should compute:
   a. return if unchanged
   b. downside break-even point
   c. return if exercised
   d. all of the above

6. In Figure 2-2, what is the result if XYZ is at 42.00 at expiration?
   a. The out-of-the-money write is superior.
   b. The in-the-money write is superior.
   c. The combined write is superior.
   d. All writes produce equal results.

7. The rolled-down position in Figure 2-3 provides all of the following benefits **EXCEPT**:
    a. additional downside protection
    b. additional income if the stock price stabilizes
    c. greater maximum profit potential
    d. additional income if the stock price rises slightly

8. Which of the following is a drawback of rolling up?
    a. Downside break-even point is raised.
    b. Debits are incurred.
    c. Loss potential is increased.
    d. All of the above.

9. If XYZ cv Pfd A is quoted "converts into 25 shares at a price of 10," how many shares of the underlying stock must you purchase to cover one call?
    a. 2
    b. 4
    c. 10
    d. 250

10. Which of the following statements is **NOT** true about writing covered calls against warrants?
    a. The warrants must be paid for in full.
    b. The transaction must be a cash transaction.
    c. The investor must deposit 50% of the value of the warrants.
    d. The warrants have no loan value.

ANSWER SHEET

MATCHING QUIZ

A.	9	**F.**	7
B.	4	**G.**	8
C.	10	**H.**	3
D.	2	**I.**	6
E.	1	**J.**	5

FILL-INS

1. The primary objective of covered writing is <u>increased income through stock ownership</u>. (Page 42)
2. An investment position that offers less risk generally has <u>lower reward potential</u>. (Page 44)
3. The return if unchanged is also called the <u>static return</u>. (Page 49)
4. When commissions are taken into account, the more shares an investor writes against, the <u>higher</u> the returns and the <u>lower</u> the break-even point will be. (Page 54)
5. Writing half of the position against in-the-moneys and half against out-of-the-moneys on the same stock is called a <u>combined write</u>. (Page 66)
6. Rolling down generally reduces the <u>maximum profit potential</u> of a position. (Page 72)
7. Simultaneously buying one call and selling another results in a <u>spread</u> position. (Page 76)
8. When an investor <u>rolls up</u>, a debit is incurred. (Page 80)
9. A convertible security that has been called by the company trades at the <u>call price</u>. (Page 90)
10. The key to successfully implementing the incremental return strategy is to <u>roll for credits</u>. (Page 92)

MULTIPLE CHOICE

1. **b** See page 39 of the text.
2. **a** See page 41 of the text.
3. **d** See page 42 of the text. Outright stock ownership will only outperform covered writing if the stock increases in price substantially during the life of the call.

4.   **c**   See page 45 of the text. Investors using this strategy are willing to have the stock called away if necessary to meet their objectives.

5.   **d**   See page 47 of the text.

6.   **d**   See page 67 of the text.

7.   **c**   See page 73 of the text. When a stock is falling, additional downside protection is often more important than maximum profit potential.

8.   **d**   See page 80 of the text. The debit required raises the break-even point and subjects the writer to a potential loss if the stock should pull back.

9.   **b**   See page 88 of the text. Note that the price is irrelevant to the conversion calculation.

10.   **c**   See page 90 of the text.

Call Buying

READING ASSIGNMENT

Chapter 3 of the text.

OBJECTIVES

By the end of this lesson, you should be able to:

Assess the risk and reward of a prospective call buying situation.

Lock in profits.

Take defensive action in the event of a relatively small move in price.

KEY TERMS

bull spread, 113
calendar spread, 116
delta, 99
hedge ratio, 99
intermediate-term call, 98
option pricing curve, 99
rolling down, 112
spread, 112

CHALLENGE

MATCHING QUIZ

Match each term in the left column with a definition from the right column, by placing the number of the definition in the space next to the term.

_____	**A.** calendar spread	**1.** Another name for delta.
_____	**B.** delta	**2.** Being long one call and short a different call on a stock at the same time.
_____	**C.** hedge ratio	**3.** Closing part of a position and replacing it with another option to create a new position.
_____	**D.** rolling	**4.** Buying a call and at the same time selling another call with the same striking price but a shorter expiration date.
_____	**E.** spread	**5.** The amount by which a call will increase or decrease in price if the underlying stock moves by 1 point.
_____	**F.** intermediate term call	**6.** A means for a call buyer to lower the break-even point by creating a bull spread.
_____	**G.** rolling down	**7.** Offers moderate amount of risk/reward.

FILL-INS

Fill in the blank(s) with the correct word(s) or phrase(s).

1. The time value premium of a call is highest when the stock is

   _____.

2. Call option rankings for buying purposes must be based on the
   _____ of the underlying stocks.

3. The strategy of rolling down to a bull spread has the effect of
   _____ the break-even point for a position.

4. The call option pricing curve depicts the relationship between the price of
   the call and its _____.

5. In general, rolling up or down to a spread requires that the investor have
   a _____ account.

6. The success of call buying depends on the ability to
    _____ and
    _____.

7. A speculator employs call buying because of its _____.

8. The _____ changes every time the underlying stock changes even fractionally in price.

9. If the holder of an intermediate- or long-term call sells a near-term call with the same striking price as the call already owned, a _____ _____ has been created.

10. In the option pricing curve, the near-, intermediate-, and long-term curves are nearer the intrinsic value line where? _____

MULTIPLE CHOICE

Circle the letter of the correct answer.

1. The investor who buys a call:
    a. can margin the entire price.
    b. must deposit 50% of the call purchase price.
    c. must pay for the call in full.
    d. none of the above.

2. Call buyers normally profit when the underlying stock:
    a. remains the same
    b. rises in price
    c. drops in price
    d. any of the above

3. An option with a lower delta is most suitable for:
    a. long-term trading
    b. short-term trading
    c. day trading
    d. margin trading

4. The call purchaser's position on the underlying stock should be:
    a. neutral
    b. bearish
    c. bullish
    d. any of the above

5. The strategy of selling a call the investor is currently long and buying another call at the next higher striking price is called:
 a. calendar spread
 b. rolling down
 c. bull spread
 d. rolling up

Refer to the following graph for questions 6–9:

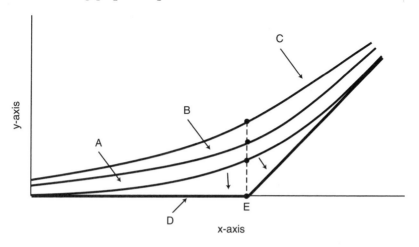

6. The y-axis and x-axis are, respectively:
 a. Option price and striking price
 b. Stock price and striking price
 c. Option price and stock price
 d. Option price and intrinsic value

7. Curve C is the:
 a. Long-term price curve.
 b. Intermediate-term price curve.
 c. Short-term price curve.
 d. Intrinsic value.

8. The vertical dashed line (E) represents the:
 a. Price curve.
 b. Stock price.
 c. Expiration date.
 d. Striking price.

9. The dog-leg curve (D) represents:
    a. Long-term price curve.
    b. Intermediate-term price curve.
    c. Short-term price curve.
    d. Intrinsic value.

10. One should not normally invest more than how much of total risk capital in call buying?
    a. 85%
    b. 50%
    c. 25%
    d. 15%

ANSWER SHEET

MATCHING QUIZ

       A. 4
       B. 5
       C. 1
       D. 3
       E. 2
       F. 7
       G. 6

FILL-INS

1. The time value premium of a call is highest when the stock is <u>at the striking price of the call</u>. (Page 99)
2. Call option rankings for buying purposes must be based on the <u>volatilities</u> of the underlying stocks. (Page 103)
3. The strategy of rolling down to a bull spread has the effect of <u>lowering</u> the break-even point for a position. (Page 113)
4. The call option pricing curve depicts the relationship between the price of the call and its <u>intrinsic value</u>. (Page 99)
5. In general, rolling up or down to a spread requires that the investor have a <u>margin</u> account. (Page 117)
6. The success of call buying depends on the ability to <u>select stocks that will go up in price</u> and <u>time the selection reasonably well</u>. (Page 95)
7. A speculator employs call buying because of its <u>leverage</u>. (Page 95)
8. The <u>delta</u> changes every time the underlying stock changes even fractionally in price. (Page 100)
9. If the holder of an intermediate- or long-term call sells a near-term call with the same striking price as the call already owned, a <u>calendar spread</u> has been created. (Page 116)
10. In the option pricing curve, the near-, intermediate-, and long-term curves are nearer the intrinsic value line where? <u>At the ends</u> (Page 99)

MULTIPLE CHOICE

1.   **c**   See page 95 of the text.
2.   **b**   See page 97 of the text.
3.   **a**   See pages 101–103 of the text. The shorter-term the strategy, the higher the delta of the option should be.
4.   **c**   See page 97 of the text. Call buyers normally profit only if the underlying stock rises in price.
5.   **d**   See page 109 of the text.
6.   **c**   See page 99 of the text.
7.   **a**   See page 99 of the text.
8.   **d**   See page 99 of the text.
9.   **d**   See page 99 of the text.
10. **d**   See page 96 of the text.

Other Call Buying Strategies

READING ASSIGNMENT

Chapter 4 of the text.

OBJECTIVES

By the end of this lesson, you should be able to:

Implement a protected short sale (synthetic put).

Implement a reverse hedge (simulated straddle).

KEY TERMS

protected short sale, 118
reverse hedge, 123
straddle, 123
synthetic put, 118
trading against the straddle, 126

CHALLENGE

MATCHING QUIZ

Match each term in the left column with a definition from the right column, by placing the number of the definition in the space next to the term.

_____ **A.** protected short sale

1. Simultaneously buying a call and a put on the same underlying stock.

_____ **B.** reverse hedge

2. Purchasing a call at the same time one is short the underlying stock.

_____ **C.** simulated combination

3. Selling calls or stock to take the profits from one side of a position.

_____ **D.** straddle buy

4. Selling stock short and buying two calls with different striking prices.

_____ **E.** trading against the straddle

5. Purchasing calls on more shares than one has sold short.

FILL-INS

Fill in the blank(s) with the correct word(s) or phrase(s).

1. Another name for a protected short sale is a _____.

2. The strategy called a simulated straddle is the _____.

3. The effect of buying a call against a short sale of stock is to
   _____.

4. The downside break-even point for a reverse hedge is equal to the
   _____ minus the _____ of the position.

5. A reverse hedge can be made more bullish or bearish by
   _____.

6. To determine the maximum risk when you protect a short sale by buying a call option, use the formula

   Risk = _____ + _____ − _____

7. As protection for a short sale, buy a call that is either _____-the-money or only slightly _____-the-money.

8. The reverse hedge has limited/unlimited loss potential and limited/unlimited profit potential.

9. Before expiration, in a reverse hedge, profits can sometimes be made close to the striking price because some _____ is left in the purchased calls.

MULTIPLE CHOICE

Circle the letter of the correct answer.

1. The maximum loss in a reverse hedge position occurs when the stock price at expiration is:
   a. above the striking price
   b. below the striking price
   c. near the striking price
   d. exactly at the striking price

2. The maximum risk of a protected short sale equals the striking price of the purchased call:
   a. plus call price minus stock price
   b. minus call price minus stock price
   c. plus call price plus stock price
   d. minus call price plus stock price

3. Short sales of stock that are protected by long calls are margined at normal rates if the stock is:
   a. above the strike price
   b. below the strike price
   c. at the strike price
   d. none of the above

4. The margin requirement for a reverse hedge is the purchase price of the calls plus:
   a. 10% of the underlying stock price
   b. 20% of the underlying stock price
   c. 50% of the underlying stock price
   d. 100% of the underlying stock price

5. Adjusting the ratio of long calls to short stock so that the break-even
    points are equidistant from the current stock price creates a:
    a. bullish position
    b. bearish position
    c. neutral position
    d. maximum profit position

Refer to the following graph for questions 6–7.

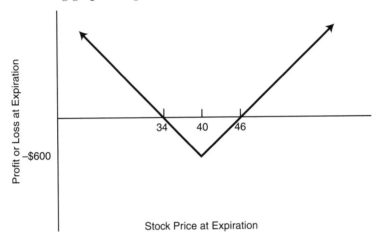

6. The graph represents:
    a. The option pricing curve.
    b. A reverse hedge (simulated straddle).
    c. A protected short sale.
    d. None of the above.

7. The –$600 represents:
    a. The minimum loss if the stock is at the striking price at expiration,
        including the cost of dividends on the underlying stock.
    b. The minimum loss if the stock is at the striking price at expiration,
        excluding the cost of dividends on the underlying stock.
    c. The maximum loss if the stock is at the striking price at expiration,
        including the cost of dividends on the underlying stock.
    d. The maximum loss if the stock is at the striking price at expiration,
        excluding the cost of dividends on the underlying stock.

Refer to the following graph for questions 8–9.

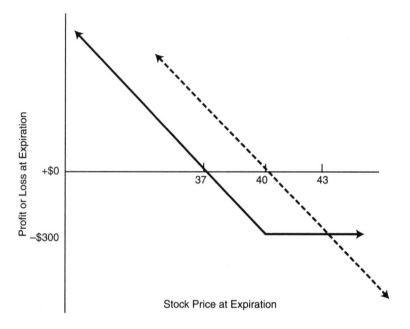

8. The solid line represents:
   a. The option pricing curve.
   b. A reverse hedge (simulated straddle).
   c. A protected short sale.
   d. None of the above.

9. The dashed line represents:
   a. A short sale.
   b. Price of the underlying security.
   c. Intrinsic value.
   d. Profit or loss at expiration.

10. For a protected short sale, the margin requirement is:
    a. 10% of the call's striking price plus any out-of-the-money amount.
    b. 30% of the current short stock's market value.
    c. 50% of the underlying stock's value.
    d. Both a and b.

ANSWER SHEET

MATCHING QUIZ

 A. 2
 B. 5
 C. 4
 D. 1
 E. 3

FILL-INS

1. Another name for a protected short sale is a <u>synthetic put</u>. (Page 118)
2. The strategy called a simulated straddle is the <u>reverse hedge</u>. (Page 123)
3. The effect of buying a call against a short sale of stock is to <u>limit the risk to a fixed amount</u>. (Page 118)
4. The downside break-even point for a reverse hedge is equal to the <u>striking price</u> minus the <u>maximum risk</u> of the position. (Page 125)
5. A reverse hedge can be made more bullish or bearish by <u>altering the ratio of long calls to short stock</u>. (Page 128)
6. To determine the maximum risk when you protect a short sale by buying a call option, use the formula

   Risk = <u>Striking price of purchased call</u> + <u>Call price</u> – <u>Stock price</u> (Page 119)

7. As protection for a short sale, buy a call that is either <u>at</u>-the-money or only slightly <u>out-of</u>-the-money. (Page 120)
8. The reverse hedge has <u>limited</u>/unlimited loss potential and limited/<u>unlimited</u> profit potential. (Page 123)
9. Before expiration, in a reverse hedge, profits can sometimes be made close to the striking price because some <u>time value premium</u> is left in the purchased calls. (Page 125)

MULTIPLE CHOICE

1. **d** See page 123 of the text.
2. **a** See page 119 of the text.
3. **b** See page 121 of the text.
4. **c** See page 124 of the text. In calculating the margin requirement, remember that the short sale is marked to the market, so the requirement increases if the stock rises in price.

5. **c** See pages 128–130 of the text.
6. **b** See page 124 of the text.
7. **d** See page 123 of the text.
8. **c** See page 120 of the text.
9. **a** See page 120 of the text.
10. **a** See page 121 of the text.

Naked Call Writing

READING ASSIGNMENT

Chapter 5 of the text.

OBJECTIVES

By the end of this lesson, you should be able to:

Understand the investment required for an uncovered (naked) call option strategy.

Understand the psychological requirements of an uncovered (naked) call option strategy.

Assess the risk and reward of an uncovered (naked) call option strategy.

KEY TERMS

kicker, 136
naked (uncovered) call, 133
rolling for credits, 140–144

CHALLENGE

MATCHING QUIZ

Match each term in the left column with a definition from the right column, by placing the number of the definition in the space next to the term.

_____ **A.** kicker

_____ **B.** naked call write

_____ **C.** rolling for credits

1. Selling a call option without owning the underlying stock or an equivalent security.

2. Buying back calls when the stock reaches the next higher striking price and selling new calls for credit at the higher striking price.

3. Maintenance requirement applied against each naked call write.

FILL-INS

Fill in the blank(s) with the correct word(s) or phrase(s).

1. Another term for a naked call is _____.

2. A naked write loses money if the stock advances _____.

3. The margin requirement for a naked call is _____ percent of the stock price, plus the _____, less the amount by which the stock is below the _____.

4. "Time value premium" is heavily influenced by the _____ estimate of the stock.

5. If the stock price moves up, the naked write will necessarily/not necessarily lose money.

6. Some brokers have a requirement, called a _____, that a maintenance requirement be applied against each option written naked.

7. Selling naked options is a high/low risk strategy.

8. Writing a naked out-of-the-money call offers a high/low probability of making a small/large profit.

9. Instead of shorting stock for a few points of movement, you can use a deeply _____-the-money naked write.

10. In most cases, naked call writing is used as a deeply _____-the-money strategy.

MULTIPLE CHOICE

Circle the letter of the correct answer.

1. Naked option positions are marked to the market:
   a. hourly
   b. daily
   c. weekly
   d. monthly

2. The most favorable options for writing naked calls are:
   a. stock options
   b. futures options
   c. index options
   d. LEAPS options

3. The minimum margin required for a naked write is:
   a. 5% of the stock price
   b. 10% of the stock price
   c. 15% of the stock price
   d. 20% of the stock price

4. The strategy of rolling for credits involves writing calls that are:
   a. at-the-money
   b. in-the-money
   c. out-of-the-money
   d. any of the above

5. The two requirements for successfully implementing the strategy of rolling for credits are:
   a. The volatility increases and the investor has sufficient margin.
   b. The volatility decreases and the investor has sufficient margin.
   c. The stock continues rising and the investor has sufficient margin.
   d. The stock stops rising and the investor has sufficient margin.

Refer to the following graph for questions 6–8.

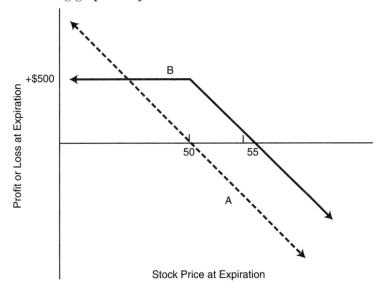

6. The solid line has the configuration of a:
   a. Short sale of stock.
   b. Naked call write.
   c. Roll for credit.
   d. None of the above.

7. The solid line (B) represents the:
   a. Naked write.
   b. Short sale.
   c. Time value premium.
   d. Profit or loss at expiration.

8. The dashed line (A) represents the:
   a. Naked write.
   b. Short sale.
   c. Time value premium.
   d. Profit or loss at expiration.

9. To write a naked call, you need to put up:
   a. Cash only.
   b. Collateral only.
   c. Both cash and collateral.
   d. None of the above.

10. Writing at-the-money calls when the stock price is initially close to the striking price of the written call is:
    a. Normally required by the broker.
    b. The correct defensive action to limit risk.
    c. Not widely utilized.
    d. Preferable to rolling for credits.

ANSWER SHEET

MATCHING QUIZ

        A. 3
        B. 1
        C. 2

FILL-INS

1. Another term for a naked call is <u>uncovered write</u>. (Page 133)
2. A naked write loses money if the stock advances <u>by more than the amount of time value premium in the call</u>. (Page 133)
3. The margin requirement for a naked call is <u>20</u> percent of the stock price, plus the <u>call premium</u>, less the amount by which the stock is below the <u>striking price</u>. (Page 135)
4. "Time value premium" is heavily influenced by the <u>volatility</u> estimate of the stock. (Page 132)
5. If the stock price moves up, the naked write will necessarily/<u>not necessarily</u> lose money. (Page 133)
6. Some brokers have a requirement, called a <u>kicker</u>, that a maintenance requirement be applied against each option written naked. (Page 136)
7. Selling naked options is a <u>high</u>/low risk strategy. (Page 137)
8. Writing a naked out-of-the-money call offers a <u>high</u>/low probability of making a <u>small</u>/large profit. (Page 138)
9. Instead of shorting stock for a few points of movement, you can use a deeply <u>in</u>-the-money naked write. (Page 139)
10. In most cases, naked call writing is used as a deeply <u>out-of</u>-the-money strategy. (Page 144)

MULTIPLE CHOICE

1.   **b**   See page 136 of the text. Investors should monitor naked positions closely, to avoid being taken out of a position prematurely by an unexpected margin call.
2.   **c**   See page 138 of the text. This is because gaps in trading prices are rare in indices.
3.   **b**   See page 135 of the text.

4. **a** See page 140 of the text. The strategy is rarely used by individual investors because of the large collateral requirements.

5. **d** See page 141 of the text.

6. **b.** See page 134 of the text.

7. **a.** See page 134 of the text.

8. **b.** See page 134 of the text.

9. **b.** See page 136 of the text.

10. **c** See page 140 of the text.

Ratio Call Writing

READING ASSIGNMENT

Chapter 6 of the text.

OBJECTIVES

By the end of this lesson, you should be able to:

Explain ratio writing.
Understand the investment required for ratio writing.
Explain the variable ratio write.
Describe the basic concept of a spread.

KEY TERMS

CHALLENGE

MATCHING QUIZ

Match each term in the left column with a definition from the right column, by placing the number of the definition in the space next to the term.

_____ **A.** equivalent stock position (ESP)

_____ **B.** profit range

_____ **C.** ratio call writing

_____ **D.** spread

_____ **E.** variable ratio write

_____ **F.** splitting the quote

_____ **G.** vertical spread

_____ **H.** diagonal spread

_____ **I.** horizontal spread

_____ **J.** neutral ratio

1. Buying one call option and selling another on the same underlying stock but with different terms.

2. Selling both an in- and an out-of-the-money call for each 100 shares of the underlying stock.

3. Position delta.

4. Span between the downside and upside break-even points for a position.

5. Selling calls against more shares of the underlying stock than one owns.

6. Calls having different expiration dates and different striking prices.

7. Calls having the same striking price but different expiration dates.

8. Calls having the same expiration date but different striking prices.

9. Executing at a price between the current bid and asked prices.

10. Determined by dividing the delta of the written call into 1.

FILL-INS

Fill in the blank(s) with the correct word(s) or phrase(s).

1. The margin requirements for a ratio write are the sum of the requirements for a _____ and a _____.

2. The ratio writing strategy is the opposite of the _____ strategy.

3. Another name for a variable ratio write is _____.

4. An investor can automatically convert a ratio write to a covered write or a naked write by using _____.

5. A _____ position is a hedged position in which at least two securities are used.

6. The ratio write is a combination of _____ call writing and _____ call writing.

7. In a 2:1 ratio write, the formula for computing the points of maximum profit is:

Points of maximum profit = _____ − _____ + 2 × _____

8. To roll down a ratio write, you would buy back the written calls and write calls at a lower _____ _____.

9. To determine the correct ratio in a ratio-adjusting strategy, you can use the _____.

10. When you simultaneously buy one option and sell another, you create a _____.

MULTIPLE CHOICE

Circle the letter of the correct answer.

1. A spread in which the calls involved have the same expiration date but different striking prices is a:
    a. vertical spread
    b. horizontal spread
    c. diagonal spread
    d. trapezoidal spread

2. A spread in which the calls involved have the same striking price but different expiration dates is a:
    a. vertical spread
    b. horizontal spread
    c. diagonal spread
    d. trapezoidal spread

3. The item(s) that must be specified when placing a spread order is (are):
    a. the options being bought and sold
    b. the price at which the order is to be executed
    c. whether the price is a debit or a credit
    d. all of the above

4. To determine the neutral ratio for a written call:
    a. Divide the delta of the call into 1.
    b. Multiply the delta of the call by 1.
    c. Add 1 to the delta of the call.
    d. Subtract 1 from the delta of the call.

5. A position with an ESP of 0 is:
    a. bullish
    b. bearish
    c. neutral
    d. none of the above

Refer to the following graph for questions 6–7.

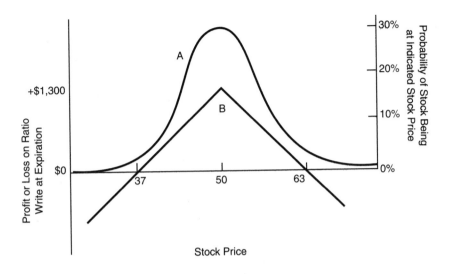

6. Line A represents:
   a. Profit on a ratio write.
   b. A stock price probability curve.
   c. A variable ratio write.
   d. Both a and b.

7. Line B represents:
   a. A ratio write profit graph.
   b. A profitability curve associated with a naked write.
   c. The maximum potential loss on a naked write.
   d. The probability of profit on a naked write.

Refer to the following graph for questions 8–10.

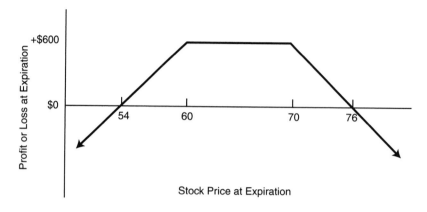

8. The graph represents:
   a. Profit on a ratio write.
   b. A stock price probability curve.
   c. Profit on a variable ratio write.
   d. Both b and c.

9. On the x-axis, 76 represents the:
   a. Point of maximum profit.
   b. Downside break-even point.
   c. Upside break-even point.
   d. Point of maximum loss.

10. On the y-axis, $600 represents the:
    a. Maximum cost of the position.
    b. Maximum profit on the position.
    c. Upside break-even point.
    d. Minimum profit on the position.

ANSWER SHEET

MATCHING QUIZ

      A. 3
      B. 4
      C. 5
      D. 1
      E. 2
      F. 9
      G. 8
      H. 6
      I. 7
      J. 10

FILL-INS

1. The margin requirements for a ratio write are the sum of the requirements for a naked write and a covered write. (Page 150)
2. The ratio writing strategy is the opposite of the reverse hedge strategy. (Page 154)
3. Another name for a variable ratio write is trapezoidal hedge. (Page 155)
4. An investor can automatically convert a ratio write to a covered write or a naked write by using good-until-canceled stop orders. (Page 164)
5. A delta-neutral position is a hedged position in which at least two securities are used. (Page 167)
6. The ratio write is a combination of covered call writing and naked call writing. (Page 146)
7. In a 2:1 ratio write, the formula for computing the points of maximum profit is:

Points of maximum profit = Strike price – Stock price + 2 × Call price (Page 152)

8. To roll down a ratio write, you would buy back the written calls and write calls at a lower striking price. (Page 158)
9. To determine the correct ratio in a ratio-adjusting strategy, you can use the delta. (Page 160)
10. When you simultaneously buy one option and sell another, you create a spread. (Page 168)

MULTIPLE CHOICE

1. **a** See page 169 of the text.
2. **b** See page 169 of the text.
3. **d** See page 170 of the text. To determine the price at which the order should be executed, it is necessary to know the bid and asked prices of the options involved.
4. **a** See page 154 of the text.
5. **c** See page 163 of the text.
6. **b** See page 149 of the text.
7. **a** See page 149 of the text.
8. **c** See page 157 of the text.
9. **c** See page 157 of the text.
10. **b** See page 157 of the text.

Bull Spreads

READING ASSIGNMENT

Chapter 7 of the text.

OBJECTIVES

By the end of this lesson, you should be able to:

Explain the degrees of aggressiveness in a bull spread.

Identify situations in which a bull spread strategy is appropriate.

Implement a bull spread.

KEY TERMS

bull spread, 172
call bull spread, 172

CHALLENGE

MATCHING QUIZ

Match each term in the left column with a definition from the right column, by placing the number of the definition in the space next to the term.

_____   **A.** least aggressive bull spread   **1.** Stock is well below the higher
                                                          striking price.

_____   **B.** aggressive bull spread   **2.** Debit transaction.

_____   **C.** most aggressive bull spread   **3.** Both calls are out-of-the-money.

_____   **D.** call bull spread   **4.** Both calls are in-the-money.

FILL-INS

Fill in the blank(s) with the correct word(s) or phrase(s).

1. A call bull spread is always a _____ transaction.

2. The maximum credit that can be recovered from a bull spread is the amount that is equal to _____.

3. The investment required to establish a bull spread is the _____ plus _____.

4. _____ may represent a significant percentage of the profit and net investment.

5. Aggressive bull spreads are most attractive when the underlying common stock is close to/far from the lower striking price when the spread is established.

6. The longer it takes the underlying stock to advance, the more/less advantage swings to the spread.

MULTIPLE CHOICE

Circle the letter of the correct answer.

1. A bull spread is a:
   a. horizontal spread
   b. vertical spread
   c. diagonal spread
   d. trapezoidal spread

Refer to the following graph for questions 2–3.

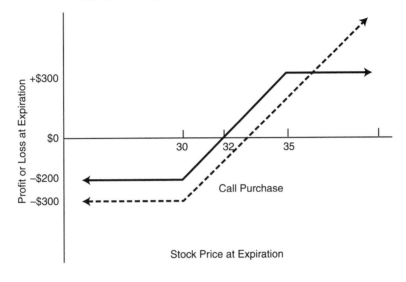

2. Which statement is true?
   a. The graph represents how to lower the break-even point on a common stock.
   b. All bull spreads have profit graphs with this shape when the expiration dates are the same for both calls.
   c. Not all bull spread profit graphs look like this, even when the expiration dates are the same for both calls.
   d. All bull spreads have profit graphs with this shape when the expiration dates are different for both calls.

3. The graph shows that the break-even point for the bull spread is:
   a. 35.
   b. 30.
   c. 32.
   d. Cannot tell.

Refer to the following graph for questions 4–5.

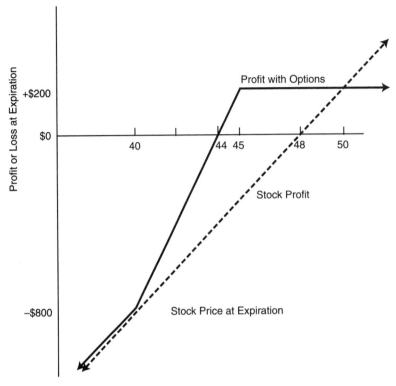

4. By utilizing options, the break-even point is lowered:
    a. From 50 to 48.
    b. From 48 to 45.
    c. From 50 to 44.
    d. From 48 to 44.

5. The option position outperforms the original stock position when the stock stabilizes where?
    a. Anywhere above 50.
    b. Anywhere below 40.
    c. Between 40 and 50.
    d. Between 44 and 48.

ANSWER SHEET

MATCHING QUIZ

        A. 4
        B. 1
        C. 3
        D. 2

FILL-INS

1. A call bull spread is always a <u>debit</u> transaction. (Page 172)
2. The maximum credit that can be recovered from a bull spread is the amount that is equal to <u>the difference between the striking prices</u>. (Page 179)
3. The investment required to establish a bull spread is the <u>net debit</u> plus <u>commissions</u>. (Page 174)
4. <u>Commissions</u> may represent a significant percentage of the profit and net investment. (Page 174)
5. Aggressive bull spreads are most attractive when the underlying common stock is <u>close to</u>/far from the lower striking price when the spread is established. (Page 175)
6. The longer it takes the underlying stock to advance, the <u>more</u>/less advantage swings to the spread. (Page 178)

MULTIPLE CHOICE

1.   **b** See page 172 of the text.
2.   **b** See page 173 of the text.
3.   **c** See pages 173–174 of the text.
4.   **d** See page 181 of the text.
5.   **c** See pages 182–183 of the text.

Bear Spreads Using Call Options

READING ASSIGNMENT

Chapter 8 of the text.

OBJECTIVES

By the end of this lesson, you should be able to:
    Compare a bear spread with a bull spread.
    Select and implement a bull spread.

KEY TERMS

call bear spread, 186

CHALLENGE

MATCHING QUIZ

Match each term or phrase in the left column with a definition or corresponding phrase from the right column, by placing the number of the definition in the space next to the term.

_____ **A.** call bear spread

1. In a call bear spread, the net credit received.

_____ **B.** maximum profit potential

2. In a call bear spread, lower striking price plus credit.

_____ **C.** break-even point

3. Buy a call at one striking price and sell another at a lower striking price.

FILL-INS

Fill in the blank(s) with the correct word(s) or phrase(s).

1. A bear spread tends to be profitable if the underlying stock _____ in price.

2. A bear spread strategist realizes the maximum profit when the stock drops in price and both options _____.

3. The basic option strategy is to sell _____ and buy _____.

4. In a call bear spread, you buy a call at a certain striking price and sell a call at a higher/lower striking price.

5. A large credit bear position is usually a(n) aggressive/defensive position.

MULTIPLE CHOICE

Circle the letter of the correct answer.

1. When set up with call options, a bear spread is a:
   a. debit transaction
   b. neutral transaction
   c. credit transaction
   d. profitable transaction

2. A bear spread is a:
   a. vertical spread
   b. horizontal spread
   c. diagonal spread
   d. trapezoidal spread

Refer to the following graph for questions 3–4.

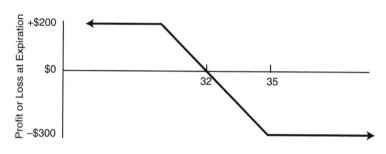

Stock Price at Expiration

3. The break-even point is:
   a. 30.
   b. 32.
   c. 35.
   d. Not shown.

4. This position becomes profitable when the stock moves:
   a. Below 30.
   b. Below 32.
   c. Between 32 and 35.
   d. Over 35.

5. In a call bear spread, the maximum risk equals:
   a. Difference in striking prices – credit received + commissions.
   b. Collateral investment required.
   c. Net credit received.
   d. Both a and b.

ANSWER SHEET

MATCHING QUIZ

      A. 3

      B. 1

      C. 2

FILL-INS

1. A bear spread tends to be profitable if the underlying stock <u>declines</u> in price. (Page 186)
2. A bear spread strategist realizes the maximum profit when the stock drops in price and both options <u>expire worthless</u>. (Page 187)
3. The basic option strategy is to sell <u>time value</u> and buy <u>intrinsic value</u>. (Page 189)
4. In a call bear spread, you buy a call at a certain striking price and sell a call at a higher/<u>lower</u> striking price. (Page 186)
5. A large credit bear position is usually a(n) <u>aggressive</u>/defensive position. (Page 189)

MULTIPLE CHOICE

1.   **c** See page 186 of the text.
2.   **a** See page 186 of the text.
3.   **b** See page 188 of the text.
4.   **b** See page 187 of the text.
5.   **d** See page 188 of the text.

Calendar Spreads

READING ASSIGNMENT

Chapter 9 of the text.

OBJECTIVES

By the end of this lesson, you should be able to:

Explain the calendar spread.

Implement both a neutral and a bullish calendar spread.

KEY TERMS

CHALLENGE

MATCHING QUIZ

Match each term or phrase in the left column with a definition or corresponding phrase from the right column, by placing the number of the definition in the space next to the term.

_____	**A.** neutral calendar spread	**1.** Buying a calendar spread.
_____	**B.** bullish calendar spread	**2.** A call calendar spread established when the underlying price is far below the striking price.
_____	**C.** antivolatility strategy	**3.** Calendar spread.
_____	**D.** time spread	**4.** Calendar spread established when underlying price is at or near the striking price.

FILL-INS

Fill in the blank(s) with the correct word(s) or phrase(s).

1. Another term for a calendar spread is _____.

2. As volatility increases, the spread _____; as volatility decreases, the spread _____.

3. The investment required to establish a calendar spread is the _____ plus_____ .

4. Risk is limited to the _____ spent to establish the spread, plus commission.

5. The easiest and most conservative type of downside defensive action is _____.

MULTIPLE CHOICE

Circle the letter of the correct answer.

1. A calendar spread is a:
   a. horizontal spread
   b. vertical spread
   c. diagonal spread
   d. none of the above

2. A calendar spread is established by:
   a. selling a near-term call and buying an intermediate-term call
   b. selling a near-term call and buying a long-term call
   c. selling an intermediate-term call and buying a long-term call
   d. any of the above

3. A calendar spread is neutral if, when it is established, the underlying stock is:
   a. below the striking price of the options
   b. above the striking price of the options
   c. at or near the striking price of the options
   d. either above or below the striking price of the options

Refer to the following graph for questions 4–5.

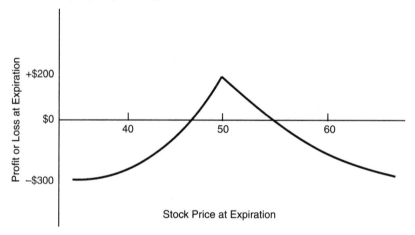

4. In this graph:
   a. The spread is profitable between 46 and 55.
   b. The maximum possible loss is $300.
   c. At 40 or 60, there is some time premium left.
   d. All of the above.

ANSWER SHEET

MATCHING QUIZ

> **A.** 4
> **B.** 2
> **C.** 1
> **D.** 3

FILL-INS

1. Another term for a calendar spread is <u>time spread</u>. (Page 191)
2. As volatility increases, the spread <u>widens</u>; as volatility decreases, the spread <u>shrinks</u>. (Page 194)
3. The investment required to establish a calendar spread is the <u>net debit</u> plus <u>commissions</u>. (Page 191)
4. Risk is limited to the <u>original debit</u> spent to establish the spread, plus commission. (Page 192)
5. The easiest and most conservative type of downside defensive action is <u>to do nothing</u>. (Page 195)

MULTIPLE CHOICE

1. **a** See page 191 of the text.
2. **d** See page 198 of the text.
3. **c** See page 192 of the text. The investor establishing a calendar spread is selling time, rather than predicting the direction of the stock.
4. **d** See pages 193–194.

The Butterfly Spread

READING ASSIGNMENT

Chapter 10 of the text.

OBJECTIVES

By the end of this lesson, you should be able to:
    Explain the butterfly spread.
    Implement and take follow-up action on the butterfly spread.

KEY TERMS

    butterfly spread, 200
    smallest-debit butterfly spread, 203

CHALLENGE

MATCHING QUIZ

Match each term or phrase in the left column with a definition or corresponding phrase from the right column, by placing the number of the definition in the space next to the term.

_____	**A.** butterfly spread	**1.** Butterfly spread in which the stock is some distance away from the middle striking price.
_____	**B.** smallest-debit butterfly spread	**2.** Net debit of butterfly spread.
_____	**C.** net investment	**3.** Neutral position combining a bull and a bear spread.
_____	**D.** upside break-even	**4.** Highest strike – net debit.

FILL-INS

Fill in the blank(s) with the correct word(s) or phrase(s).

1. The maximum profit in a butterfly spread is realized at the _____ of the written calls.

2. The risk in a butterfly spread is equal to the _____.

3. The smallest-debit butterfly spread is one in which the stock price is some distance away from _____.

4. The butterfly spread involves one/two/three striking prices.

5. The downside break-even is limited to the _____ strike + _____.

MULTIPLE CHOICE

Circle the letter of the correct answer.

1. The number of striking prices involved in establishing a butterfly spread is:
    a. 2
    b. 3
    c. 4
    d. 6

2. The number of commissions involved in establishing a butterfly spread is:
   a. 2
   b. 3
   c. 4
   d. 8

3. A butterfly spread is:
   a. neutral
   b. bullish
   c. bearish
   d. riskless

4. The margin required for a butterfly spread is:
   a. 20% of the call price
   b. 20% of the stock price
   c. the difference between the striking prices
   d. the net debit expended

Refer to the following graph for question 5.

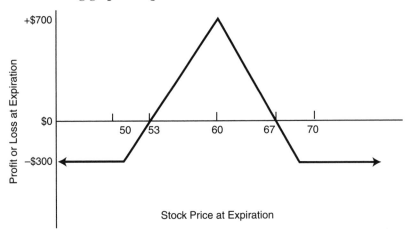

5. In this graph:
   a. The spread is profitable between 53 and 67.
   b. The maximum possible loss is theoretically infinite.
   c. The maximum profit is at 67.
   d. None of the above.

ANSWER SHEET

MATCHING QUIZ

   A. 3
   B. 1
   C. 2
   D. 4

FILL-INS

1. The maximum profit in a butterfly spread is realized at the <u>striking price</u> of the written calls. (Page 200)
2. The risk in a butterfly spread is equal to the <u>net debit required</u>. (Page 201)
3. The smallest-debit butterfly spread is one in which the stock price is some distance away from <u>the middle striking price</u>. (Page 203)
4. The butterfly spread involves one/two/<u>three</u> striking prices. (Page 200)
5. The downside break-even is limited to the <u>lowest</u> strike + <u>net debit</u>. (Page 201)

MULTIPLE CHOICE

1. **b**   See page 200 of the text. Two calls will be sold at the same (middle) striking price.
2. **c**   See page 200 of the text. A total of four options are purchased to establish the position.
3. **a**   See page 200 of the text.
4. **d**   See page 201 of the text. This is the same as the risk in the spread.
5. **a**   See pages 201–202 of the text.

Ratio Call Spreads

READING ASSIGNMENT

Chapter 11 of the text.

OBJECTIVES

By the end of this lesson, you should be able to:
> Explain the ratio spread.
> Implement and take follow-up action on the ratio spread.

KEY TERMS

> delta spread, 216
> ratio call spread, 210

CHALLENGE

MATCHING QUIZ

Match each term or phrase in the left column with a definition or corresponding phrase from the right column, by placing the number of the definition in the space next to the term.

_____	**A.** ratio call spread	**1.**	Number of calls bought versus number of calls sold.
_____	**B.** delta spread	**2.**	Buy calls at one price, sell more calls at a higher strike.
_____	**C.** ratio	**3.**	Deltas are used to set up and monitor the spread.

FILL-INS

Fill in the blank(s) with the correct word(s) or phrase(s).

1. The maximum profit at expiration for a ratio spread is realized if the stock is _____.

2. For margin purposes, a ratio call spread is really the combination of a _____ and a _____.

3. To determine the correct ratio to use in a delta spread, divide _____ by _____.

4. In a ratio call spread, profit or loss at expiration is _____ below the lower striking price.

5. The greatest risk in a ratio call spread is on the upside/downside.

6. Delta spreads are aggressive/neutral/defensive spreads.

MULTIPLE CHOICE

Circle the letter of the correct answer.

1. The greatest risk in a ratio spread occurs when the stock price:
   a. rises
   b. falls
   c. stays the same
   d. either a or b

2. The profit or loss at expiration for a ratio spread:
    a. is constant below the higher striking price
    b. is constant above the higher striking price
    c. is constant below the lower striking price
    d. is constant above the lower striking price.

3. A ratio spread is:
    a. bullish
    b. neutral
    c. bearish
    d. riskless

Refer to the following graph for question 4.

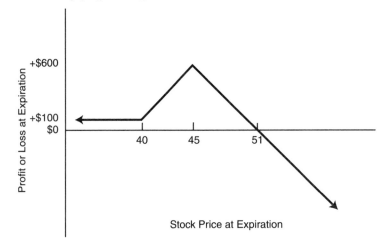

4. In this graph:
    a. The maximum potential profit is $100.
    b. The maximum potential profit occurs at 45.
    c. The break-even point is at 40.
    d. The maximum potential loss is $100.

5. In a ratio spread, the upside break-even point is equal to:
    a. Initial credit + difference between strikes.
    b. Difference between strikes – initial debit.
    c. Higher strike price + points of maximum profit.
    d. Higher strike price – points of maximum profit.

ANSWER SHEET

MATCHING QUIZ

 A. 2
 B. 3
 C. 1

FILL-INS

1. The maximum profit at expiration for a ratio spread is realized if the stock is exactly at the striking price of the written options. (Page 211)
2. For margin purposes, a ratio call spread is really the combination of a bull spread and a naked call write. (Page 212)
3. To determine the correct ratio to use in a delta spread, divide the delta of the purchased call by the delta of the written call. (Page 217)
4. In a ratio call spread, profit or loss at expiration is constant below the lower striking price. (Page 210)
5. The greatest risk in a ratio call spread is on the upside/downside. (Page 211)
6. Delta spreads are aggressive/neutral/defensive spreads. (Page 216)

MULTIPLE CHOICE

1. **a** See page 211 of the text.
2. **c** See page 210 of the text. This is because both options would be worthless in that area.
3. **b** See page 210 of the text. The loss to the upside may theoretically be unlimited.
4. **b** See page 211 of the text.
5. **c** See page 211 of the text.

Combining Calendar and Ratio Spreads

READING ASSIGNMENT

Chapter 12 of the text.

OBJECTIVES

By the end of this lesson, you should be able to:

Explain the combined use of calendar and ratio spreads.

Implement and take follow-up action on these spreads.

KEY TERMS

delta-neutral calendar spread, 227
in-the-money calendar spread, 228
ratio calendar spread, 222

CHALLENGE

Match each term or phrase in the left column with a definition or corresponding phrase from the right column, by placing the number of the definition in the space next to the term.

_____   **A.** ratio calendar spread

1. The shorter-term call has a higher delta than the longer-term call.

_____   **B.** in-the-money calendar spread

2. Divide the delta of the long call by the delta of the short call.

_____   **C.** delta-neutral calendar spread

3. Sell near-term calls, buy fewer intermediate- or long-term calls.

FILL-INS

Fill in the blank(s) with the correct word(s) or phrase(s).

1. The collateral requirement for a ratio calendar spread is
   _____ less _____.

2. Margin calls are possible on a ratio calendar spread because the naked calls are _____.

3. To determine the ratio of calls for a delta-neutral calendar spread, divide _____ by _____.

4. To get to a defensive action point, always leave enough _____.

5. In a ratio calendar spread, if the stock never rises above the striking price, there is a large probability of a large/small profit.

MULTIPLE CHOICE

Circle the letter of the correct answer.

1. To establish a ratio calendar spread, an investor:
   a. Buys near-term calls and sells a larger number of intermediate- or long-term calls.
   b. Buys near-term calls and sells a smaller number of intermediate- or long-term calls.
   c. Sells near-term calls and buys a larger number of intermediate- or long-term calls.
   d. Sells near-term calls and buys a smaller number of intermediate- or long-term calls.

2. As time passes, the break-even point for a ratio calendar spread:
   a. increases
   b. decreases
   c. remains the same
   d. either a or b

3. Which statement is true for in-the-money calls?
   a. A shorter-term call has a lower delta than a longer-term call.
   b. A shorter-term call has the same delta as a longer-term call.
   c. A shorter-term call has a higher delta than a longer-term call.
   d. None of the above.

4. If in a ratio calendar spread the stock rises above the striking price after the near-term call expires:
   a. There is a large probability of a small profit.
   b. There is a small probability of a small loss if defensive action is taken.
   c. There is a good probability of a large profit.
   d. The spread can no longer generate a profit.

5. A ratio calendar spread should be closed if the stock price:
   a. Breaks out above technical resistance.
   b. Breaks out below a support level.
   c. Breaks out above the eventual break-even point at expiration.
   d. Both a and b.

ANSWER SHEET

MATCHING QUIZ

        A. 3

        B. 2

        C. 1

FILL-INS

1. The collateral requirement for a ratio calendar spread is <u>the margin required for the naked calls</u> less <u>the credit taken in</u>. (Page 223)
2. Margin calls are possible on a ratio calendar spread because the naked calls are <u>marked to market</u>. (Page 223)
3. To determine the ratio of calls for a delta-neutral calendar spread, divide <u>the delta of the long call</u> by <u>the delta of the short call</u>. (Page 227)
4. To get to a defensive action point, always leave enough <u>collateral</u>. (Page 223)
5. In a ratio calendar spread, if the stock never rises above the striking price, there is a large probability of a large/<u>small</u> profit. (Page 226)

MULTIPLE CHOICE

1.   **d**   See page 222 of the text.
2.   **a**   See page 225 of the text.
3.   **c**   See page 228 of the text.
4.   **c**   See page 227 of the text. Once the stock rises above the striking price after the near-term call expires, there is a *good* probability of large profits (i.e., a small probability event – that the stock can rise above the strike – has already happened).
5.   **d**   See page 226 of the text.

Reverse Spreads

READING ASSIGNMENT

Chapter 13 of the text.

OBJECTIVES

By the end of this lesson, you should be able to:

Explain reverse calendar and ratio spreads.
Implement and take follow-up action on these spreads.

KEY TERMS

CHALLENGE

FILL-INS

Fill in the blank(s) with the correct word(s) or phrase(s).

1. Reverse calendar spreads are infrequently used because of the
    _____ involved.

2. Another name for a reverse ratio call spread is a _____.

3. It is best to establish a reverse calendar spread using a stock that is

    _____.

4. In a backspread, you sell a call at one striking price and buy several calls
    at a higher/lower striking price.

5. In a reverse ratio spread, the investment is relatively small because there
    are no _____.

MULTIPLE CHOICE

Circle the letter of the correct answer.

1. To establish a reverse calendar spread, the investor:
    a. Sells a short-term call option and buys a higher-priced call option.
    b. Sells a long-term call option and buys a lower-priced call option.
    c. Sells a short-term call option and buys a longer-term call option.
    d. Sells a long-term call option and buys a shorter-term call option.

2. In a backspreading strategy, the investor would like the underlying stock
    to:
    a. Move up slightly.
    b. Move down slightly.
    c. Move either up or down substantially.
    d. Remain stable.

3. The maximum loss at expiration for a reverse ratio spread is realized:
    a. at the striking price of the purchased call
    b. at the striking price of the sold call
    c. below the striking price of the purchased call
    d. below the striking price of the sold call

Refer to the following graph for questions 4–5.

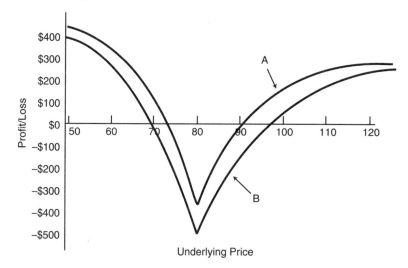

4. In this graph of a reverse calendar spread, curve A reflects profit and loss points if implied volatility:
   a. Falls prior to expiration of the near-term options.
   b. Remains unchanged.
   c. Increases prior to expiration of the near-term options.
   d. Goes negative.

5. In the graph, curve B indicates that:
   a. The spread becomes profitable if the stock price rises above 98.
   b. The spread is profitable at any price between 70 and 98.
   c. The spread becomes profitable if the stock price falls below 70.
   d. Both a and c.

ANSWER SHEET

FILL-INS

1. Reverse calendar spreads are infrequently used because of the <u>margin requirements</u> involved. (Page 230)
2. Another name for a reverse ratio call spread is a <u>backspread</u>. (Page 232)
3. It is best to establish a reverse calendar spread using a stock that is <u>volatile</u>. (Page 231)
4. In a backspread, you sell a call at one striking price and buy several calls at a <u>higher</u>/lower striking price. (Page 232)

5. In a reverse ratio spread, the investment is relatively small because there are no <u>naked calls</u>. (Page 233)

MULTIPLE CHOICE

1. **d** See page 230 of the text. The calls have the same striking price.
2. **c** See page 232 of the text.
3. **a** See page 233 of the text.
4. **a** See page 232 of the text.
5. **d** See page 231 of the text.

Diagonalizing a Spread

READING ASSIGNMENT

Chapter 14 of the text.

OBJECTIVES

By the end of this lesson, you should be able to:

Explain how to diagonalize a spread.

Implement and take follow-up action on these spreads.

KEY TERMS

CHALLENGE

Match each term or phrase in the left column with a definition or corresponding phrase from the right column, by placing the number of the definition in the space next to the term.

_____   **A.**   diagonal backspread

1. Buy a longer-term call at a lower striking price, sell a near-term call at a higher striking price.

_____   **B.**   diagonal bear spread

2. Different striking prices, different expiration dates

_____   **C.**   diagonal bull spread

3. Buy more than one longer-term call against the short-term call sold.

_____   **D.**   diagonal spread

4. Sell a call with a lower striking price and nearer expiration, buy a call with a higher striking price and more distant expiration date.

FILL-INS

Fill in the blank(s) with the correct word(s) or phrase(s).

1. Buying a call and selling another call at a higher striking price but with the same expiration date is a _____.

2. Buying a longer-term call and selling a near-term call at a higher striking price is a _____.

3. Buying a longer-term call and selling a near-term call with a lower striking price is a _____.

4. A spread in which the credits equal the debits when the position is established is called _____.

MULTIPLE CHOICE

Circle the letter of the correct answer.

1. A diagonal spread involves:
   a. different striking prices and the same expiration date
   b. same striking price and different expiration dates
   c. different striking prices and different expiration dates
   d. different stock prices and different expiration dates

2. The maximum profit at expiration for a diagonal spread is realized when the stock is:
   a. near the striking price of the written call
   b. near the striking price of the purchased call
   c. above the striking price of the written call
   d. above the striking price of the purchased call

3. To establish a diagonal backspread, an investor would:
   a. Sell a call with a higher strike and buy more calls at a lower strike.
   b. Sell a call with a lower strike and buy more calls at a higher strike.
   c. Sell a near-term call and buy more longer-term calls.
   d. Sell a longer-term call and buy more near-term calls.

ANSWER SHEET

MATCHING QUIZ

A. 3
B. 4
C. 1
D. 2

FILL-INS

1. Buying a call and selling another call at a higher striking price but with the same expiration date is a <u>vertical call bull spread</u>. (Page 236)
2. Buying a longer-term call and selling a near-term call at a higher striking price is a <u>diagonal bull spread</u>. (Page 237)
3. Buying a longer-term call and selling a near-term call with a lower striking price is a <u>diagonal bear spread</u>. (Page 239)
4. A spread in which the credits equal the debits when the position is established is called <u>an even-money spread</u>. (Page 240)

MULTIPLE CHOICE

1. **c** See page 236 of the text.
2. **a** See page 238 of the text. The diagonal spread gives up a small portion of potential upside profits in order to provide a hedge to the downside.
3. **b** See page 240 of the text. In this strategy, the short call reduces the risk of owning the longer-term calls if the price of the underlying stock falls.

Put Option Basics

READING ASSIGNMENT

Chapter 15 of the text.

OBJECTIVES

By the end of this lesson, you should be able to:

Understand the fundamentals of put strategies.

Explain the effects on put option strategies of dividends, exercise and assignment, and conversion.

KEY TERMS

conversion, 253
reversal, 254

CHALLENGE

Match each term or phrase in the left column with a definition or corresponding phrase from the right column, by placing the number of the definition in the space next to the term.

_____	**A.** reversal	**1.** An arbitrage position involving buying the underlying stock, buying a put option for the stock and selling a call at the same striking prices.
_____	**B.** dividend	**2.** An arbitrage position involving selling a put, buying a call, and shorting the underlying stock.
_____	**C.** conversion	**3.** The larger it is, the more valuable the put.

FILL-INS

Fill in the blank(s) with the correct word(s) or phrase(s).

1. The buyer of a put hopes that stock prices will _____.

2. A put is in-the-money when the underlying stock is _____; it is out-of-the-money when the underlying stock is _____.

3. The time value premium of a put is greatest when the stock is _____.

4. An in-the-money put loses time value _____ than an in-the-money call.

5. If the underlying stock pays a dividend, it has the effect of _____ the value of the puts.

6. The put writer who is assigned must _____.

7. Shorting the underlying stock while selling a put and buying a call at the same strike is called _____.

8. The holder of a put exercises the option by _____.

9. In addition to the amount a stock declines below the striking price and the time remaining until expiration, the frequency of assignment for a put option is also affected by the _____.

10. Time value premium equals put option price plus stock price minus _____.

MULTIPLE CHOICE

Circle the letter of the correct answer.

1. As the price of the underlying stock declines, a put:
   a. decreases in value.
   b. increases in value.
   c. maintains its original value.
   d. expires.

2. The time value premium of an option is always:
   a. excess value less intrinsic value
   b. excess value less striking price
   c. excess value above its intrinsic value
   d. excess value over striking price

3. When the underlying stock is at the strike price:
   a. Calls will sell for more than puts.
   b. Calls will sell for less than puts.
   c. Calls and puts will sell for the same price.
   d. Puts will not be available.

4. A conversion position has:
   a. neutral risk
   b. low risk
   c. high risk
   d. no risk

5. To establish a conversion position, an arbitrageur buys 100 shares of the underlying stock and:
   a. Buys 2 puts and sells 1 call at the same striking price.
   b. Buys 1 put and sells 2 calls at different striking prices.
   c. Buys 1 put and sells 1 call at the same striking price.
   d. Buys 1 put and sells 1 call at different striking prices.

Refer to the following graph for questions 6–7.

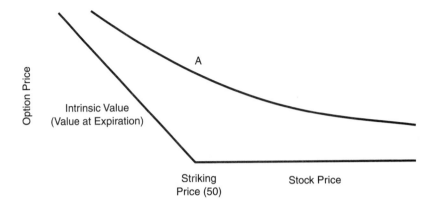

6. In the graph, curve A represents:
   a. A call option price curve.
   b. The decline in intrinsic value as the option nears expiration.
   c. The increase in stock price.
   d. The put option price curve.

7. The intrinsic value line in the graph:
   a. Reflects a gain in value as the stock falls below the striking price.
   b. Reflects a loss in value as the stock falls below the striking price.
   c. Faces in the opposite direction of the call option pricing curve.
   d. Both a and c.

8. As the ex-dividend date of a stock nears, the time value premium of in-the-money puts on the stock will:
   a. Remain unaffected.
   b. Tend to equal or exceed the dividend payment.
   c. Decline by the amount of the dividend payment.
   d. Behave in the same way as for a call option.

9. An in-the-money put option:
   a. Loses time value premium faster than a call option.
   b. Gains time value premium faster than a call option.
   c. Gains and loses time value premium in the same way a call option does.
   d. None of the above.

ANSWER SHEET

MATCHING QUIZ

        A. 2

        B. 3

        C. 1

FILL-INS

1. The buyer of a put hopes that stock prices will <u>decline</u>. (Page 245)
2. A put is in-the-money when the underlying stock is <u>below the strike price</u>; it is out-of-the-money when the underlying stock is <u>above the striking price</u>. (Page 246)
3. The time value premium of a put is greatest when the stock is <u>at the striking price</u>. (Page 247)
4. An in-the-money put loses time value <u>more quickly</u> than an in-the-money call. (Page 247)
5. If the underlying stock pays a dividend, it has the effect of <u>increasing</u> the value of the puts. (Page 248)
6. The put writer who is assigned must <u>receive stock</u>. (Page 250)
7. Shorting the underlying stock while selling a put and buying a call at the same strike is called <u>reversal or reverse conversion</u>. (Page 254)
8. The holder of a put exercises the option by <u>selling stock at the striking price</u>. (Page 250)
9. In addition to the amount a stock declines below the striking price and the time remaining until expiration, the frequency of assignment for a put option is also affected by the <u>dividend payment</u>. (Page 252)
10. Time value premium equals put option price plus stock price minus <u>striking price</u>. (Page 246)

MULTIPLE CHOICE

1.   **b**   See page 246 of the text. This is the opposite of a call's price action.
2.   **c**   See page 246 of the text.
3.   **a**   See page 247 of the text. This occurs because of the cost of carrying stock.
4.   **d**   See page 254 of the text.
5.   **c**   See page 254 of the text. Although conversions are riskless, it is not always possible to establish a profitable conversion.
6.   **d**.   See page 249 of the text.
7.   **d**   See page 248 of the text.
8.   **b**   See page 252 of the text.
9.   **a**   See page 255 of the text.

Put Option Buying

READING ASSIGNMENT

Chapter 16 of the text.

OBJECTIVES

By the end of this lesson, you should be able to:

Explain the basics of put option buying.

Compare put buying and the short sale.

Implement a put buying strategy and follow-up action.

KEY TERMS

calendar spread, 269

equivalent positions, 270

rolling up, 267

CHALLENGE

MATCHING QUIZ

Match each put buying follow-up strategy in the left column with a definition from the right column, by placing the number of the definition in the space next to the term.

_____ **A.** liquidate

_____ **B.** do nothing

_____ **C.** roll down

_____ **D.** spread

_____ **E.** combine

1. Sell an out-of-the-money put against a put already held.

2. Continue to hold a long put.

3. Sell a long put for a profit and do not reinvest.

4. Buy a call at a lower strike while holding a put.

5. Sell a long put, pocket the initial investment, and invest the remaining proceeds in out-of-the-money puts at a lower strike.

FILL-INS

Fill in the blank(s) with the correct word(s) or phrase(s).

1. A put option purchase is an alternative to _____.

2. Even if the underlying stock rises in price, a put buyer has _____ risk.

3. The rolling up strategy is most attractive when _____.

4. Of the five put buying follow-up strategies, the one that never turns out to be the worst choice is _____.

5. An investor can determine whether two strategies are equivalent by comparing their _____.

MULTIPLE CHOICE

Circle the letter of the correct answer.

1. A put purchase is used for speculative purposes when:
    a. The investor expects a decline in the underlying stock's price.
    b. The investor expects a rise in the underlying stock's price.
    c. The investor has no opinion on the underlying stock's price.
    d. A put purchase is always speculative.

2. Compared to an in-the-money-put, an out-of-the-money put offers:
   a. lower reward and lower risk
   b. lower reward and higher risk
   c. higher reward and higher risk
   d. higher reward and lower risk

3. The delta of a put ranges between:
   a. minus 1 and plus 1
   b. 0 and plus 1
   c. minus 1 and minus 10
   d. 0 and minus 1

4. The rolling up spread has which effect?
   a. Risk is increased; the break-even point is raised.
   b. Risk is not increased; the break-even point is raised.
   c. Risk is increased; the break-even point is lowered.
   d. Risk is not increased; the break-even point is lowered.

5. Two investment positions are considered equivalent when:
   a. They have the same time value premium.
   b. They have the same cash requirements.
   c. They have the same profit potential.
   d. They have the same break-even point.

Refer to the following graph for question 6.

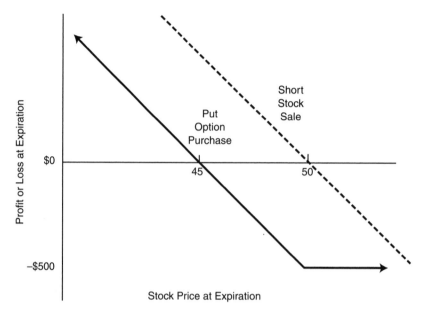

6. The graph represents a put option purchase compared to a short sale. Which statement is true?

   a. Both strategies involve unlimited risk.

   b. Both strategies involve limited risk.

   c. The put option purchase obligates the holder to pay dividends on the underlying stock.

   d. The put option purchase involves more limited risk than the short sale.

ANSWER SHEET

MATCHING QUIZ

A. 3
B. 2
C. 5
D. 1
E. 4

FILL-INS

1. A put option purchase is an alternative to <u>the short sale of stock</u>. (Page 256)
2. Even if the underlying stock rises in price, a put buyer has <u>limited</u> risk. (Page 256)
3. The rolling up strategy is most attractive when <u>the debit involved to create the spread is small</u>. (Page 267)
4. Of the five put buying follow-up strategies, the one that never turns out to be the worst choice is <u>the spread tactic</u>. (Page 265)
5. An investor can determine whether two strategies are equivalent by comparing their <u>profit graphs</u>. (Page 270)

MULTIPLE CHOICE

1. **a** See page 256 of the text.
2. **c** See page 258 of the text.
3. **d** See page 261 of the text. That is, the delta of a put equals the delta of a similar call minus 1.
4. **b** See page 268 of the text. However, this strategy also has the effect of reducing the profit potential of the position.
5. **c** See page 270 of the text. Many call strategies have equivalent put strategies.
6. **d** See pages 257–258 of the text.

Put Buying in Conjunction with Common Stock Ownership

READING ASSIGNMENT

Chapter 17 of the text.

OBJECTIVES

By the end of this lesson, you should be able to:

Explain how put buying works in conjunction with common stock ownership.

Implement a put buying strategy as protection in a covered call situation.

KEY TERM

collar strategy, 278

CHALLENGE

FILL-INS

Fill in the blank(s) with the correct word(s) or phrase(s).

1. A long put/long stock strategy is equivalent to _____.

2. The purchase of a put in conjunction with a covered call write is termed a _____.

3. The strategy of protecting a covered call write with a put purchase is equivalent to a _____.

4. The put is like an insurance policy with a(n) infinite/finite life.

5. The purchase of an out-of-the-money put offers more/less downside protection than an at- or in-the-money put.

MULTIPLE CHOICE

Circle the letter of the correct answer.

1. Put purchases can be used:
   a. to limit upside risk on a stock that is shorted
   b. to limit downside loss on a stock that is shorted
   c. to maximize upside profit on a stock that is owned
   d. to limit downside loss on a stock that is owned

2. A short-term holder of stock who buys a put eliminates the holding period on the stock. The holding period begins again when:
   a. The put is sold.
   b. The stock is sold.
   c. The put expires.
   d. Both a and c are true.

3. An investor can eliminate the risk of large losses on a covered write and still maintain a profitable position on the upside by purchasing:
   a. an in-the-money put
   b. an at-the-money put
   c. an out-of-the-money put
   d. an out-of-the-money call

Refer to the following graph for questions 4–5.

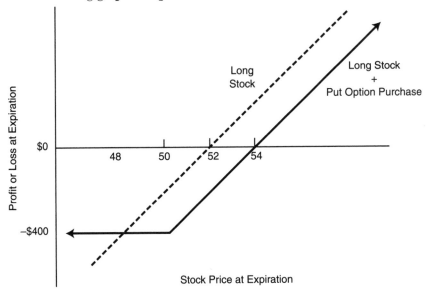

4. The graph represents a long stock position protected by a put option purchase compared to a long position in the underlying stock. Which statement is true?
   a. Both strategies involve unlimited risk.
   b. Both strategies involve potentially infinite losses.
   c. The put option purchase limits the risk of the long position.
   d. Both a and b.

5. The stock owner buys the put for 2 points, which allows him to sell the stock at 50. He buys the stock at 52. The maximum loss on this position is:
   a. 2 points.
   b. 4 points.
   c. 6 points.
   d. unlimited.

ANSWER SHEET

FILL-INS

1. A long put/long stock strategy is equivalent to <u>a call purchase</u>. (Page 274)
2. The purchase of a put in conjunction with a covered call write is termed a <u>protective collar, or just "collar."</u> (Page 275)
3. The strategy of protecting a covered call write with a put purchase is equivalent to a <u>bull spread</u>. (Page 278)
4. The put is like an insurance policy with a(n) infinite/<u>finite</u> life. (Page 271)
5. The purchase of an out-of-the-money put offers more/<u>less</u> downside protection than an at- or in-the-money put. (Page 273)

MULTIPLE CHOICE

1. **d** See page 271 of the text. This position is also known as a synthetic long call.
2. **d** See page 275 of the text. The holding period begins when the put is sold *or* expires.
3. **c** See page 276 of the text. Note, though, that the money spent for the put purchase will reduce the overall return from the covered write.
4. **c** See pages 271–272 of the text.
5. **b** See pages 271–272 of the text.

Buying Puts in Conjunction with Call Purchases

READING ASSIGNMENT

Chapter 18 of the text.

OBJECTIVES

By the end of this lesson, you should be able to:

Explain how put buying works in conjunction with call purchases.
Implement and follow up on a straddle.

KEY TERMS

CHALLENGE

MATCHING QUIZ

Match each put buying strategy in the left column with a definition from the right column, by placing the number of the definition in the space next to the term.

_____	**A.** straddle	**1.** If the stock rises enough to make a straddle profitable to the upside, sell the underlying stock short.
_____	**B.** strangle	**2.** Buy the underlying stock and two puts.
_____	**C.** reverse hedge with puts	**3.** A put and a call with the same terms and underlying stock.
_____	**D.** trading against the straddle	**4.** A put and a call with different terms.

FILL-INS

Fill in the blank(s) with the correct word(s) or phrase(s).

1. Straddle buying is equivalent to a _____.

2. Buying the underlying stock and buying two put options is called a _____.

3. A straddle buyer should consider rolling up when _____.

4. Buying a put in conjunction with calls locks in profits and offers further/no further potential appreciation.

5. In a straddle, the probability of losing your entire investment is great/moderate/small.

MULTIPLE CHOICE

Circle the letter of the correct answer.

1. A straddle purchase involves buying a put and a call with:
   a. same underlying stock, different striking prices, and same expiration date
   b. same underlying stock, same striking price, and same expiration date
   c. different underlying stocks, same striking price, and same expiration date
   d. same underlying stock, same striking price, and different expiration dates

2. A strangle purchase involves buying a put and a call with:
   a. same expiration date, different striking prices
   b. same expiration date, same striking price
   c. different expiration dates, different striking prices
   d. different expiration dates, same striking price

3. The probability of losing one's entire initial investment is large for a:
   a. reverse hedge
   b. straddle buy
   c. reverse hedge with puts
   d. strangle buy

Refer to the following graph for question 4.

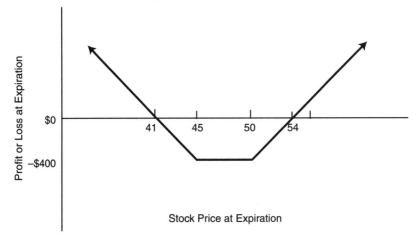

4. The graph represents:
   a. A strangle purchase.
   b. A straddle purchase.
   c. A reverse hedge with puts.
   d. A trade against the straddle.

Refer to the following graph for question 5.

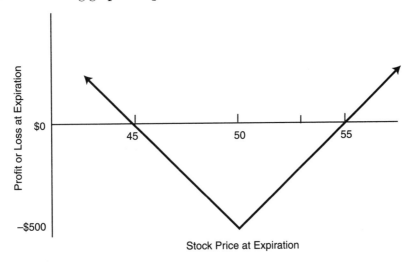

5. The graph represents:
   a. A strangle purchase.
   b. A straddle purchase.
   c. A reverse hedge with puts.
   d. A trade against the straddle.

ANSWER SHEET

MATCHING QUIZ

  A. 3
  B. 4
  C. 2
  D. 1

FILL-INS

  1. Straddle buying is equivalent to a <u>reverse hedge</u>. (Page 283)
  2. Buying the underlying stock and buying two put options is called a <u>reverse hedge with puts</u>. (Page 284)
  3. A straddle buyer should consider rolling up when <u>the underlying stock moves up to the next strike</u>. (Page 288)
  4. Buying a put in conjunction with calls locks in profits and offers <u>further</u>/no further potential appreciation. (Page 281)
  5. In a straddle, the probability of losing your entire investment is great/moderate/<u>small</u>. (Page 283)

MULTIPLE CHOICE

  1. **b** See page 282 of the text. The maximum loss is equal to the initial investment.
  2. **a** See page 288 of the text.
  3. **d** See page 291 of the text. The probability is small for a straddle.
  4. **a.** See page 290 of the text.
  5. **b.** See page 284 of the text.

The Sale of a Put

READING ASSIGNMENT

Chapter 19 of the text.

OBJECTIVES

By the end of this lesson, you should be able to:
    Explain the strategy of the uncovered put sale.
    Compare the strategies of the covered and uncovered put writes.

KEY TERMS

    covered put sale, 300
    uncovered (naked) put sale, 292

CHALLENGE

MATCHING QUIZ

Match each put selling strategy in the left column with a definition from the right column, by placing the number of the definition in the space next to the term.

_____   **A.** naked put sale   **1.** Sell a put, short the underlying stock.
_____   **B.** covered put sale   **2.** Sell a put, do not short the underlying
                                                   stock.

FILL-INS

Fill in the blank(s) with the correct word(s) or phrase(s).

1. The uncovered put writing strategy is similar to the
   _____ strategy.

2. A naked put write is aggressive if the stock price is initially
   _____.

3. For margin purposes, an investor is considered covered if the investor
   sells a put and is _____.

4. In both an uncovered put and a covered call strategy, the probability of
   achieving the maximum profit is greater if the position is established with
   the stock above/below the striking price.

5. For the naked put writer, rolling down is more/less advantageous than for
   the covered call writer.

MULTIPLE CHOICE

Circle the letter of the correct answer.

1. The collateral requirement for writing naked puts is:
   a. stock price + put premium – 20% of out-of-the-money amount
   b. stock price + 20% of put premium – out-of-the-money amount
   c. 20% of stock price + put premium – out-of-the-money amount
   d. none of the above

2. To establish a ratio put write, an investor:
   a. Sells stock short and sells 2 puts for each 100 shares of short stock.
   b. Sells stock short and sells 1 put for each 100 shares of short stock.
   c. Sells long stock and sells 2 puts for each 100 shares of short stock.
   d. Sells long stock and sells 1 put for each 100 shares of short stock.

3. A ratio put write achieves its maximum profit:
   a. at the striking price of the underlying stock
   b. above the striking price of the underlying stock
   c. below the striking price of the written options
   d. at the striking price of the written options

Refer to the following graph for questions 4–5.

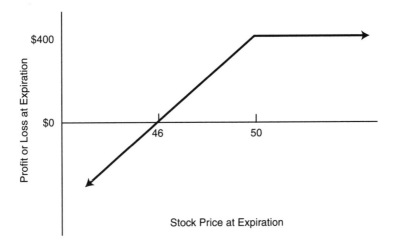

4. In the graph:
   a. The maximum profit is $400.
   b. The potential profit levels off at 50.
   c. The downside loss is limited only by the fact that the underlying stock cannot go below zero.
   d. All of the above.

5. The general configuration of the graph represents:
   a. The uncovered sale of a put.
   b. The covered sale of a put.
   c. A covered call write.
   d. Both a and c.

ANSWER SHEET

MATCHING QUIZ

A. 2

B. 1

FILL-INS

1. The uncovered put writing strategy is similar to the <u>covered call writing</u> strategy. (Page 291)
2. A naked put write is aggressive if the stock price is initially <u>below the striking price of the written option</u>. (Page 292)
3. For margin purposes, an investor is considered covered if the investor sells a put and is <u>short the underlying stock</u>. (Page 298)
4. In both an uncovered put and a covered call strategy, the probability of achieving the maximum profit is greater if the position is established with the stock <u>above</u>/below the striking price. (Pages 293–294)
5. For the naked put writer, rolling down is more/<u>less advantageous</u> than for the covered call writer. (Page 295)

MULTIPLE CHOICE

1. **c** See page 292 of the text. This is the same as the requirement for naked calls.
2. **a** See page 300 of the text.
3. **d** See page 300 of the text. This strategy has a profit graph identical to the profit graph for a ratio call write.
4. **d** See pages 292–293 of the text.
5. **d** See page 293 of the text.

The Sale of a Straddle

READING ASSIGNMENT

Chapter 20 of the text.

OBJECTIVES

By the end of this lesson, you should be able to:

Explain and compare the covered and uncovered straddle write with strangle combination writing.

Implement appropriate follow-up action.

KEY TERMS

covered straddle write, 302
equivalent stock position (ESP), 312
strangle write, 315
uncovered straddle write, 305

CHALLENGE

MATCHING QUIZ

Match each term in the left column with a definition from the right column, by placing the number of the definition in the space next to the term.

_____   **A.** covered straddle write

_____   **B.** strangle write

_____   **C.** uncovered straddle write

_____   **D.** equivalent stock position

1. The multiple of the quantity × the delta × the shares per option

2. Sell an out-of-the-money put and out-of-the-money call with stock roughly centered between the two strike prices.

3. Own the underlying stock and simultaneously write a straddle on the stock.

4. Sell the straddle without owning the underlying stock.

FILL-INS

Fill in the blank(s) with the correct word(s) or phrase(s).

1. When an investor owns the underlying stock and at the same time writes a straddle on that stock, it is referred to as a (an) _____.

2. Selling a straddle without owning the underlying stock is a (an) _____.

3. The maximum potential profit on an uncovered straddle write is realized when the stock is _____ at expiration.

4. The ESP of an option position is the multiple of the _____ times the _____ times the _____ per option.

5. Compared to a straddle writer, the strangle writer's potential profit range is _____.

MULTIPLE CHOICE

Circle the letter of the correct answer.

1. The maximum profit on a covered straddle write is:
    a. straddle premium minus striking price plus initial stock price
    b. straddle premium plus striking price minus initial stock price
    c. time value premium minus striking price plus initial stock price
    d. time value premium plus striking price minus initial stock price

2. The investment required for a naked straddle write is:
    a. 50% of the requirement on the call and the put
    b. 50% of the requirement on the call or the put
    c. the smaller of the requirement on the call or the put
    d. the greater of the requirement on the call or the put

3. To limit risk in either direction, at the same time a straddle is written, the investor should:
    a. Buy an out-of-the-money put and an out-of-the-money call.
    b. Buy an in-the-money put and an in-the-money call.
    c. Buy an at-the-money put and an at-the-money call.
    d. None of the above.

4. To establish a strangle write, an investor would:
    a. Sell an out-of-the-money put and an out-of-the-money call with the stock centered between the two strikes.
    b. Sell an in-the-money put and an in-the-money call with the stock centered between the two strikes.
    c. Sell an out-of-the-money put and an out-of-the-money call with the stock closest to the call price.
    d. Sell an in-the-money put and an in-the-money call with the stock closest to the call price.

5. Because puts lose their time value premium more quickly when they become in-the-money than calls do, an uncovered straddle or strangle write can be made more neutral initially by:
    a. buying more shares of the underlying
    b. writing extra short calls
    c. writing extra short puts
    d. none of the above

ANSWER SHEET

MATCHING QUIZ

       A. 3
       B. 2
       C. 4
       D. 1

FILL-INS

1. When an investor owns the underlying stock and at the same time writes a straddle on that stock, it is referred to as a (an) <u>covered straddle write</u>. (Page 302)
2. Selling a straddle without owning the underlying stock is a (an) <u>uncovered straddle write</u>. (Page 305)
3. The maximum potential profit on an uncovered straddle write is realized when the stock is <u>at the striking price</u> at expiration. (Page 306)
4. The ESP of an option position is the multiple of the <u>quantity</u> times the <u>delta</u> times the <u>shares</u> per option. (Page 312)
5. Compared to a straddle writer, the strangle writer's potential profit range is <u>much wider</u>. (Page 315)

MULTIPLE CHOICE

1. **b** See page 303 of the text.
2. **d** See page 306 of the text. The investor should be careful to allow sufficient collateral to avoid incurring a margin call.
3. **a** See pages 311–312 of the text. This strategy also reduces margin requirements because it eliminates naked options from the position.
4. **a** See page 315 of the text.
5. **c** See page 318 of the text. Calculating the ratio using the deltas of the options will demonstrate this.

Synthetic Stock Positions Created by Puts and Calls

READING ASSIGNMENT

Chapter 21 of the text.

OBJECTIVES

By the end of this lesson, you should be able to:

Explain and compare a synthetic long stock, a synthetic short sale, and splitting the strikes.

KEY TERMS

splitting the strikes, 325
synthetic long stock, 321
synthetic short sale, 323

CHALLENGE

MATCHING QUIZ

Match each strategy in the left column with a definition from the right column, by placing the number of the definition in the space next to the term.

_____   **A.** synthetic short sale

1. Use a lower striking price for the put and a higher one for the call.

_____   **B.** synthetic long stock

2. Buy a call, sell a put.

_____   **C.** splitting the strikes

3. Sell a call, buy a put.

FILL-INS

Fill in the blank(s) with the correct word(s) or phrase(s).

1. The position created by simultaneously buying a call and selling a put on the same stock is known as _____.

2. Simultaneously selling a call and buying a put creates a position known as _____.

3. Compared to stock ownership, the advantage of the synthetic long position is that it requires _____.

4. If an out-of-the-money put is sold naked and an out-of-the-money call purchased, the "splitting the strikes" position is said to be bullish/bearish.

5. One reason that synthetic positions are desirable over actual positions in the underlying stock is that they require _____.

MULTIPLE CHOICE

Circle the letter of the correct answer.

1. Synthetic short sales are advantageous because the investor:
   a. Does not need to borrow stock and does not require an uptick.
   b. Does not need to worry about early assignment.
   c. Does not need collateral to establish the position.
   d. Does not need to calculate a break-even point.

2. An aggressively bullish position, where profits can be made only on large upward movements by the underlying, are usually established by which method?
   a. Sell a naked in-the-money put and buy an in-the-money call.
   b. Sell a naked out-of-the-money put and buy an in-the-money call.
   c. Sell a naked in-the-money put and buy an out-of-the-money call.
   d. Sell a naked out-of-the-money put and buy an out-of-the-money call.

3. An aggressively bearish position, where profits can be made only on large declines by the underlying, are usually established by which method?
   a. Buy an in-the-money put and sell a naked in-the-money call.
   b. Buy an out-of-the-money put and sell a naked out-of-the-money call.
   c. Buy an out-of-the-money put and sell a naked out-of-the-money call.
   d. Buy an in-the-money put and sell a naked out-of-the-money call.

Refer to the following graph for question 4.

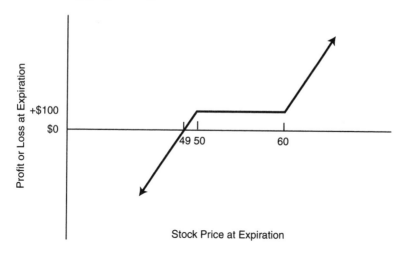

4. In the graph, which statement is **NOT** true?
   a. The position has a bullish orientation.
   b. The position has a bearish orientation.
   c. If the underlying stock is between 50 and 60 at expiration, the position generates a small profit.
   d. If the underlying rises above 60, the profit could be unlimited.

Refer to the following graph for question 5.

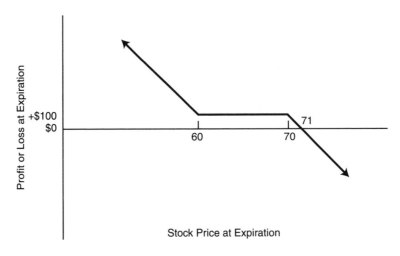

5. In the graph:
    a. If the underlying rises substantially by February expiration, large profits are possible.
    b. If the stock drops well below 70, unlimited losses are possible.
    c. If the underlying remains between 60 and 70 at expiration, the profit is equal to the initial credit.
    d. This is a bullish strategy.

ANSWER SHEET

MATCHING QUIZ

       A. 3
       B. 2
       C. 1

FILL-INS

1. The position created by simultaneously buying a call and selling a put on the same stock is known as <u>synthetic long stock</u>. (Page 321)
2. Simultaneously selling a call and buying a put creates a position known as <u>synthetic short sale</u>. (Page 323)
3. Compared to stock ownership, the advantage of the synthetic long position is that it requires <u>a much smaller investment</u>. (Page 322)
4. If an out-of-the-money put is sold naked and an out-of-the-money call purchased, the "splitting the strikes" position is said to be <u>bullish</u>/bearish. (Page 325)
5. One reason that synthetic positions are desirable over actual positions in the underlying stock is that they require <u>less investment</u>. (Pages 321, 322)

MULTIPLE CHOICE

1.   **a** See page 323 of the text. In addition, the synthetic short seller does not have to pay out dividends on the options.
2.   **d** See page 325 of the text. This strategy, though aggressive, has the potential for large profits.
3.   **c** See page 327 of the text. This strategy is often used in conjunction with stock ownership, as a "protective collar."
4.   **b** See pages 325 and 326 of the text.
5.   **c** See page 327 of the text.

Basic Put Spreads

READING ASSIGNMENT

Chapter 22 of the text.

OBJECTIVES

By the end of this lesson, you should be able to:

Explain and compare the put bear spread, the put bull spread, and the put calendar spread.

Implement and follow up on these basic spreads.

KEY TERMS

CHALLENGE

MATCHING QUIZ

Match each strategy in the left column with a definition from the right column, by placing the number of the definition in the space next to the term.

_____ **A.** put calendar spread

1. Sell a put with a lower strike price, buy a put with a higher strike price.

_____ **B.** put bear spread

2. Sell a near-term option and buy a longer-term option, both at the same strike price.

_____ **C.** put bull spread

3. Buy a put with a lower strike price, sell a put with a higher strike price.

FILL-INS

Fill in the blank(s) with the correct word(s) or phrase(s).

1. Compared to a call bear spread, a put bear spread has _____ profit potential.

2. The maximum profit in a put bull spread occurs when the underlying stock _____.

3. In a bullish put spread, the maximum loss is equal to _____.

4. The break-even price of a bullish put spread is the higher striking price less the _____.

5. A bearish calendar spread achieves the maximum profit when the near-term option _____ and the underlying stock _____ in price.

MULTIPLE CHOICE

Circle the letter of the correct answer.

1. To establish a put bear spread, an investor should:
    a. Sell a put at a higher strike and buy a put at a lower strike.
    b. Sell a put at a lower strike and buy a put at a higher strike.
    c. Sell a put with a longer expiration date and buy a put with a shorter expiration date.
    d. Sell a put with a shorter expiration date and buy a put with a longer expiration date.

2. To establish a put bull spread, an investor should:
    a. Buy a put with a longer expiration date and sell a put with a shorter expiration date.
    b. Buy a put with a shorter expiration date and sell a put with a longer expiration date.
    c. Buy a put at a higher strike and sell a put with a lower strike.
    d. Buy a put at a lower strike and sell a put with a higher strike.

3. To establish a put calendar spread, the investor should:
    a. Sell a near-term put and buy a longer-term put, both with the same strike price.
    b. Buy a near-term put and sell a longer-term put, both with the same strike price.
    c. Sell a near-term put and buy a longer-term put, with different strike prices.
    d. Buy a near-term put and sell a longer-term put, with different strike prices.

4. The maximum profit in a neutral calendar spread is realized when the stock, at expiration, is:
    a. above the striking price
    b. slightly below the striking price
    c. significantly below the striking price
    d. exactly at the striking price

Refer to the following graph for question 5.

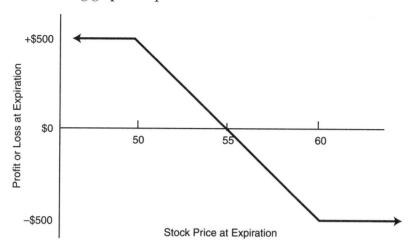

5. In the graph:
   a. The maximum profit potential is below 50.
   b. The maximum risk is anywhere below 50.
   c. The break-even point is 60.
   d. Both a and b.

ANSWER SHEET

MATCHING QUIZ

A. 2

B. 1

C. 3

FILL-INS

1. Compared to a call bear spread, a put bear spread has <u>the same</u> profit potential. (Page 330)
2. The maximum profit in a put bull spread occurs when the underlying stock <u>is at or above the higher strike price at expiration</u>. (Page 332)
3. In a bullish put spread, the maximum loss is equal to <u>the collateral requirement</u>. (Page 333)
4. The break-even price of a bullish put spread is the higher striking price less the <u>net credit</u>. (Page 333)
5. A bearish calendar spread achieves the maximum profit when the near-term option <u>expires worthless</u> and the underlying stock <u>declines</u> in price. (Page 335)

MULTIPLE CHOICE

1. **b** See page 329 of the text. The put bear spread is a debit spread.
2. **d** See page 332 of the text.
3. **a** See page 333 of the text. A calendar spread can be constructed with either puts or calls.
4. **d** See page 334 of the text. The neutral spread is established with the intention of closing it when the near-term call or put expires.
5. **a** See page 330 of the text.

Spreads Combining Calls and Puts

READING ASSIGNMENT

Chapter 23 of the text.

OBJECTIVES

By the end of this lesson, you should be able to:
   Explain and compare various spreads combining calls and puts.
   Implement and follow up on these spreads.

KEY TERMS

CHALLENGE

FILL-INS

Fill in the blank(s) with the correct word(s) or phrase(s).

1. A butterfly spread can be constructed in _____ ways, which are all equal _____.

2. A butterfly spread is the equivalent of a (an) _____.

3. A calendar straddle is a (an) _____ strategy.

4. A calendar combination is best constructed using a _____ stock, and when the striking prices of the options are_____.

5. A calendar straddle should be established when the stock price is _____.

6. The best time to establish a diagonal butterfly is _____.

7. The position that offers the possibility of owning free options is the _____.

8. The investor has the largest probability of capturing the entire near-term premium with a (an) _____.

9. The largest potential profits at near-term expiration can be realized with the _____.

10. The investor has the largest probability of losing the entire debit in a _____ position.

MULTIPLE CHOICE

Circle the letter of the correct answer.

1. A butterfly spread has which characteristics?
   a. neutral, high risk, limited profit
   b. neutral, limited risk, high profit
   c. neutral, limited risk, limited profit
   d. neutral, high risk, high profit

2. A bullish spread is constructed when the investor:
   a. Buys a call and sells a put credit spread.
   b. Buys a put and sells a call credit spread.
   c. Buys a call and sells a put debit spread.
   d. Buys a put and sells a call debit spread.

3. A bearish spread is constructed when the investor:
   a. Sells a put credit spread and buys a call.
   b. Sells a call debit spread and buys a put.
   c. Sells a call and buys a put credit spread.
   d. Sells a call credit spread and buys a put.

4. A calendar combination is made up of:
   a. a bearish out-of-the-money call calendar spread and a bullish out-of-the-money put calendar spread
   b. a bullish in-the-money call calendar spread and a bearish in-the-money put calendar spread
   c. a bullish out-of-the-money call calendar spread and a bearish out-of-the-money put calendar spread
   d. a bullish out-of-the-money put calendar spread and a bearish out-of-the-money call calendar spread

5. A calendar straddle is created when an investor:
   a. Sells a longer-term straddle and buys a near-term straddle.
   b. Sells a near-term straddle and buys a longer-term straddle.
   c. Sells a near-term straddle and buys a longer-term strangle.
   d. Sells a longer-term strangle and buys a near-term straddle.

Refer to the following graph for question 6.

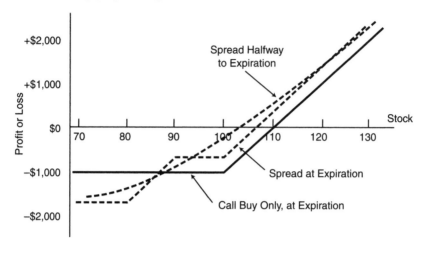

6. Which statement is not true?
   a. As long as the underlying stock does not fall below 87, the three-way spread outperforms the purchase of the call over a large range of stock prices.
   b. This is a bullish strategy.
   c. This is a call buy and put credit spread.
   d. The position does not increase risk over the purchase of the call.

ANSWER SHEET

FILL-INS

1. A butterfly spread can be constructed in <u>four</u> ways, which are all equal <u>at expiration</u>. (Pages 336–338)
2. A butterfly spread is the equivalent of a (an) <u>protected straddle write</u>. (Page 338)
3. A calendar straddle is a (an) <u>neutral</u> strategy. (Page 349)
4. A calendar combination is best constructed using a <u>relatively volatile</u> stock, and when the striking prices of the options are <u>at least 10 points apart</u>. (Page 353)
5. A calendar straddle should be established when the stock price is <u>near the striking price</u>. (Page 349)
6. The best time to establish a diagonal butterfly is <u>three to four months before near-term expiration</u>. (Page 355)
7. The position that offers the possibility of owning free options is the <u>diagonal butterfly</u>. (Page 356)
8. The investor has the largest probability of capturing the entire near-term premium with a (an) <u>calendar combination</u>. (Page 356)
9. The largest potential profits at near-term expiration can be realized with the <u>calendar straddle</u>. (Page 356)
10. The investor has the largest probability of losing the entire debit in a <u>calendar combination</u> position. (Page 357)

MULTIPLE CHOICE

1. **c** See page 336 of the text. The maximum profit is realized at the middle strike at expiration.
2. **a** See page 339 of the text.
3. **d** See page 341 of the text. This position has larger margin requirements and larger risk than an outright put purchase.
4. **c** See page 345 of the text.
5. **b** See page 348 of the text. The risk in this position is limited to the debit of the transaction, but only until the near-term options expire.
6. **d** See pages 340–341 of the text.

Ratio Spreads Using Puts

READING ASSIGNMENT

Chapter 24 of the text.

OBJECTIVES

By the end of this lesson, you should be able to:

Explain and compare the ratio put spread, the ratio put calendar spread, and the ratio calendar combination.

Implement and follow up on these spreads.

KEY TERMS

CHALLENGE

MATCHING QUIZ

Match each spread in the left column with a definition from the right column, by placing the number of the definition in the space next to the term.

_____ **A.** ratio put spread

1. Buy a longer-term put and sell a larger quantity of shorter-term puts.

_____ **B.** delta spread

2. Buy puts at one strike price and sell more puts at a lower strike price.

_____ **C.** ratio put calendar spread

3. Buy a longer-term out-of-the-money combination and sell near-term out-of-the-money combinations.

_____ **D.** ratio calendar combination

4. Used to establish and adjust neutral ratio put spreads.

FILL-INS

Fill in the blank(s) with the correct word(s) or phrase(s).

1. The best time to establish a ratio put spread is when the underlying stock price is _____.

2. To determine a neutral ratio, divide _____ by _____.

3. The investment required for a put ratio spread is the collateral requirement for a (an) _____, plus or minus the credit or debit of the position.

4. The ratio put spread has downside risk that is large and limited only by _____.

5. In a ratio calendar combination, if the near-term combination expires worthless, the longer-term combination is owned for free, and a large/modest profit could result on a substantial stock price movement in either direction.

MULTIPLE CHOICE

Circle the letter of the correct answer.

1. The downside break-even price of a ratio put spread is:
    a. higher strike price minus maximum profit potential divided by number of naked puts
    b. lower strike price minus maximum profit potential divided by number of naked puts
    c. lower strike price minus minimum profit potential divided by number of naked puts
    d. strike price differential minus maximum profit potential divided by number of naked puts

2. A ratio put calendar spread is established when an investor:
    a. Buys a longer-term put and sells two or more shorter-term puts, all with the same striking price.
    b. Buys a shorter-term put and sells two or more longer-term puts, all with the same striking price.
    c. Buys a longer-term put and sells two or more shorter-term puts, all with different striking prices.
    d. Buys a shorter-term put and sells two or more longer-term puts, all with different striking prices.

3. To establish a ratio calendar combination, an investor would:
    a. Buy a near-term out-of-the-money combination and sell several longer-term out-of-the-money combinations.
    b. Buy several longer-term out-of-the-money combinations and sell a near-term out-of-the-money combination.
    c. Buy several near-term out-of-the-money combinations and sell a longer-term out-of-the-money combination.
    d. Buy a longer-term out-of-the-money combination and sell several near-term out-of-the-money combinations.

Refer to the following graph for questions 4–5.

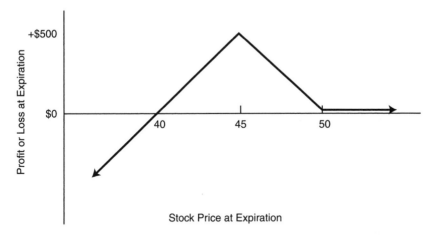

4. Which statement is **NOT** true?
   a. The profitable range is between 40 and 50.
   b. The graph reflects a ratio put spread.
   c. Losses will be generated below 40 at expiration.
   d. The maximum profit is realized if the underlying stock is at 50 at expiration.

5. Which statement is true?
   a. The upside risk is unlimited.
   b. Losses can be large.
   c. There is no downside risk.
   d. The investment consists of the collateral for a naked put, plus or minus the credit or debit of the overall position.

ANSWER SHEET

MATCHING QUIZ

        A. 2
        B. 4
        C. 1
        D. 3

FILL-INS

1. The best time to establish a ratio put spread is when the underlying stock price is <u>between the two striking prices</u>. (Page 360)
2. To determine a neutral ratio, divide <u>the delta of the put at the higher strike</u> by <u>the delta of the put at the lower strike</u>. (Page 361)
3. The investment required for a put ratio spread is the collateral requirement for a (an) <u>naked put</u>, plus or minus the credit or debit of the position. (Page 359)
4. The ratio put spread has downside risk that is large and limited only by <u>the fact that a stock cannot go below zero</u>. (Page 359)
5. In a ratio calendar combination, if the near-term combination expires worthless, the longer-term combination is owned for free, and a <u>large</u>/modest profit could result on a substantial stock price movement in either direction. (Page 364)

MULTIPLE CHOICE

1. **b** See page 359 of the text. Although the upside risk in this position is limited, the downside risk can be large.

2. **a** See page 361 of the text. The naked options involved in this position increase the collateral requirements.

3. **d** See page 364 of the text. This is a very attractive strategy, but one that must be monitored closely to avoid large losses.

4. **d** See pages 359–360 of the text.

5. **b** See page 359 of the text.

LESSON 25

LEAPS

READING ASSIGNMENT

Chapter 25 of the text.

OBJECTIVES

By the end of this lesson, you should be able to:

Explain the basic concepts and pricing of LEAPS.

Compare LEAPS with short-term options.

Implement and follow up on LEAPS-related strategies.

CHALLENGE

FILL-INS

Fill in the blank(s) with the correct word(s) or phrase(s).

1. A LEAPS is a listed call or put option that has _____.

2. The four specifications that describe an option contract are:

_____,

_____,

_____, and

_____.

3. The six factors that influence the price of an option are:

_____,

_____,

_____,

_____,

_____, and

_____.

4. The delta of an option is the amount by which the option price will change if the underlying stock _____.

5. For at-the-money options, the longer the remaining life, the _____ the option's delta.

6. A put's delta is equal to a call's delta minus _____.

7. The advantages of short LEAPS over short stock are

_____, _____, and

_____.

8. A LEAPS call with time remaining to expiration may still be assigned if it is trading _____.

9. As compared to a neutral calendar spread using shorter-term calls, to maintain a neutral calendar spread using LEAPS calls, an investor needs to buy more/fewer LEAPS calls on the long side of the spread, because of the higher/lower delta of the LEAPS calls.

MULTIPLE CHOICE

Circle the letter of the correct answer.

1. How do LEAPS differ from regular equity options?
   a. They are longer-term.
   b. They expire on the Saturday following the third Friday of the expiration month.
   c. There is no standardized striking price interval.
   d. Both a and c.

2. With respect to LEAPS pricing:
   a. The trader might think that the LEAPS is comparatively cheap or expensive, compared to a regular equity option.
   b. All the factors that influence the pricing of regular equity options influence LEAPS pricing, but in a more pronounced way.
   c. LEAPS can be in-, at-, or out-of-the-money like regular equity options.
   d. All of the above.

Refer to the following graph for question 3.

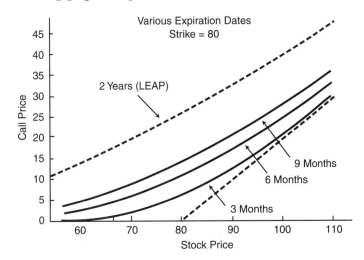

3. Which statement is true?
   a. The 2-year LEAPS sells for a little more than 4 times the 3-month option.
   b. The LEAPS is cheaper than the 3-month call.
   c. Changes in volatility have less effect on LEAPS pricing than on regular equity option pricing.
   d. The least important determinant of an option's price is the volatility of the underlying stock.

Refer to the following graph for question 4.

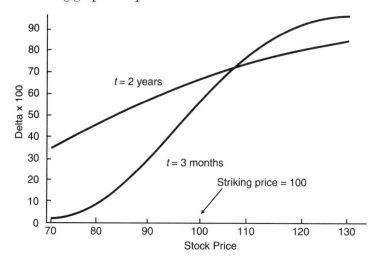

4. Which statement is true?
   a. The delta of the at-the-money LEAPS is small.
   b. The deltas of the 3-month call and the 2-year LEAPS call are about equal when the options are approximately 5% in-the-money.
   c. The delta of the 2-year LEAPS changes more dramatically when the stock moves than does the delta of the 3-month option.
   d. None of the above.

Refer to the following graph for question 5.

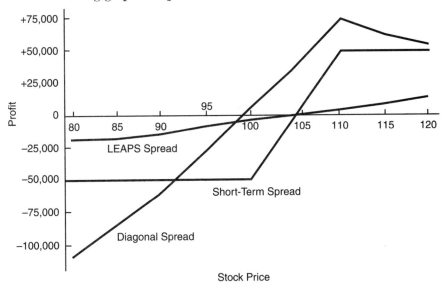

5. Which statement is true?
   a. The LEAPS spread generates most of its profit in three months' time.
   b. The maximum profit for the diagonal spread is exactly equal to the difference in the strikes.
   c. The diagonal spread is the most bearish strategy of the three in the graph.
   d. The short-term bull spread makes its maximum profit over 110.

ANSWER SHEET

FILL-INS

1. A LEAPS is a listed call or put options that has <u>two or more years of time remaining</u>. (Page 367)

2. The four specifications that describe an option contract are: <u>type (put or call)</u>, <u>underlying stock name (or symbol)</u>, <u>expiration date</u>, and <u>striking price</u>. (Page 368)

3. The six factors that influence the price of an option are: <u>underlying stock price</u>, <u>striking price,</u> <u>time remaining,</u> <u>volatility,</u> <u>risk-free interest rate,</u> and <u>dividend rate</u>. (Page 370)

4. The delta of an option is the amount by which the option price will change if the underlying stock <u>changes in price by one point</u>. (Page 387)

5. For at-the-money options, the longer the remaining life, the <u>greater</u> the option's delta. (Page 387)

6. A put's delta is equal to a call's delta minus <u>one</u>. (Page 389)

7. The advantages of short LEAPS over short stock are <u>less collateral required</u>, <u>no need to borrow stock</u>, and <u>no uptick required</u> (Page 400).

8. A LEAPS call with time remaining to expiration may still be assigned if it is trading <u>at parity</u>. (Page 401)

9. As compared to a neutral calendar spread using shorter-term calls, to maintain a neutral calendar spread using LEAPS calls, an investor needs to buy more/<u>fewer</u> LEAPS calls on the long side of the spread, because of the <u>higher</u>/lower delta of the LEAPS calls. (Page 409)

MULTIPLE CHOICE

1. **d** See pages 367 and 369 of the text.

2. **d** See pages 369–370 of the text.

3. **a.** See page 370 of the text.

4. **b** See page 387 of the text.

5. **d** See pages 404–405 of the text.

Final Examination

The purpose of this examination is to evaluate your grasp of the basic concepts and strategies. The 100 questions are all multiple choice. When you have completed the examination, compare your answers with those at the end of the book.

1. Options contracts are characterized by which of the following specifications?
   a. type, expiration date, ex-dividend date, and striking price
   b. type, underlying stock, ex-dividend date, and striking price
   c. type, underlying stock, expiration date, and striking price
   d. underlying stock, expiration date, ex-dividend date, and striking price

2. A call option is in-the-money if:
   a. The stock price is above the striking price of the option.
   b. The stock price is below the striking price of the option.
   c. The stock price is the same as the striking price of the option.
   d. The stock price is rising.

3. The expiration month code for a put option expiring in February is:
   a. Y
   b. C
   c. F
   d. N

4. Which of the following is **NOT** part of the option symbol?
   a. Base symbol
   b. Expiration month code
   c. Striking price code
   d. Underlying price

5. A covered call write loses money when:
   a. The stock rises by a distance greater than the call option premium.
   b. The stock falls by a distance greater than the call option premium.
   c. The option expires at parity.
   d. The option is called away.

6. Which of the following is **NOT** involved in the total return concept of covered writing?
   a. achieving downside protection
   b. achieving maximum potential return
   c. retaining stock ownership
   d. allowing stock to be called away

7. Which is a drawback of rolling up a covered write?
   a. Downside break-even point is raised.
   b. Debits are incurred.
   c. Loss potential is increased.
   d. All of the above.

8. When writing covered calls against warrants, which of the following statements is **NOT** true?
   a. The warrants must be paid for in full.
   b. The transaction must be a cash transaction.
   c. The investor must deposit 50% of the value of the warrants.
   d. The warrants have no loan value.

9. Normally, a call purchase is profitable when the underlying stock:
   a. remains the same
   b. rises in price
   c. drops in price
   d. any of the above

Refer to the following graph for question 10:

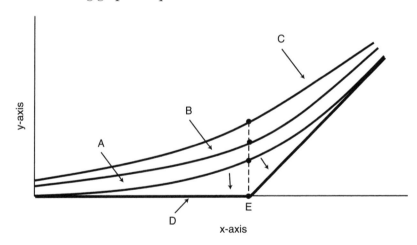

10. Which statement is **NOT** true?
    a. The y-axis and x-axis are the option price and stock price, respectively.
    b. Curve C is the long-term price curve.
    c. The dog-leg curve (D) represents the short-term price curve.
    d. The vertical dashed line (E) represents the striking price.

11. When buying calls, you should **NOT** normally invest more than how much of your total risk capital?
    a. 85%
    b. 50%
    c. 25%
    d. 15%

12. If you buy a short-term call, you:
    a. can margin the entire price.
    b. must deposit 50% of the call purchase price.
    c. must pay for the call in full.
    d. none of the above.

Refer to the following graph for question 13.

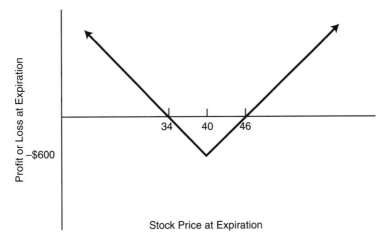

13. In the graph:
    a. The strategy is a reverse hedge (simulated straddle).
    b. The –$600 represents the minimum loss if the stock is at the striking price at expiration, excluding the cost of dividends on the underlying stock.
    c. The –$600 represents the maximum loss if the stock is at the striking price at expiration, excluding the cost of dividends on the underlying stock.
    d. Both a and c.

14. Short sales of stock protected by a long call are margined at normal rates if the stock is:
    a. above the strike price
    b. below the strike price
    c. at the strike price
    d. none of the above

15. In a reverse hedge (simulated long straddle), when you adjust the ratio of long calls to short stock so that the position delta is approximately zero, you create a:
    a. bullish position
    b. bearish position
    c. neutral position
    d. maximum profit position

16. When you protect a short sale by buying a call option, the risk is equal to:
    a. Striking price of the call + Call price + Stock price.
    b. Striking price of the call + Call price – Stock price.
    c. Striking price of the call + Call price + Margin.
    d. Striking price of the call + Call price – Margin.

17. Which statement is **NOT** true of naked option positions?
    a. They are marked to the market daily.
    b. The most favorable options for writing naked calls are index options.
    c. The minimum margin required for a naked write is 5% of the stock price.
    d. The strategy of rolling for credits involves writing calls that are at-the-money.

Refer to the following graph for question 18.

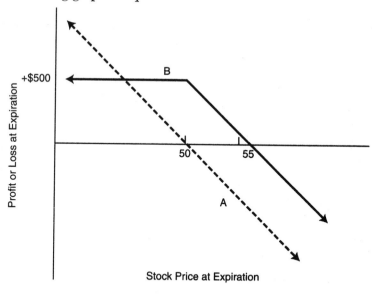

18. Which statement is true?
    a. The graph has the configuration of a short sale of a call.
    b. The solid line (B) represents the short sale of stock.
    c. The dashed line (A) represents the naked write of a put.
    d. None of the above.

19. To write a naked call, you need to put up:
    a. Cash only.
    b. Collateral only.
    c. Both cash and collateral.
    d. None of the above.

20. To successfully roll for credits, the requirements are:
    a. The volatility increases and the investor has sufficient margin.
    b. The volatility decreases and the investor has sufficient margin.
    c. The stock continues rising and the investor has sufficient margin.
    d. The stock stops rising and the investor has sufficient margin.

Refer to the following graph for question 21.

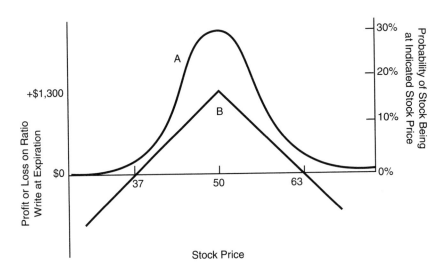

21. Which statement is true?
   a. Line B represents a profitability curve associated with a naked write.
   b. Line A represents a stock price probability curve.
   c. Line A represents the maximum potential loss on a naked write.
   d. Both a and b are true.

22. When the calls involved in a spread have the same expiration date but different striking prices, the spread is a:
   a. vertical spread
   b. horizontal spread
   c. diagonal spread
   d. trapezoidal spread

23. The item(s) that must be specified when placing a spread order is (are):
   a. the options being bought and sold
   b. the price at which the order is to be executed
   c. whether the price is a debit or a credit
   d. all of the above

24. When the calls involved in a spread have the same striking price but different expiration dates, the spread is a:
    a. vertical spread
    b. horizontal spread
    c. diagonal spread
    d. trapezoidal spread

Refer to the following graph for question 25.

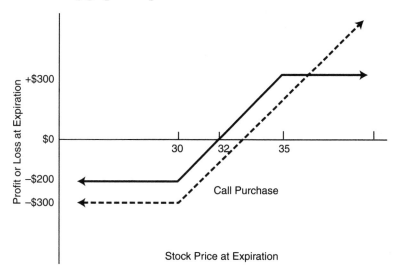

25. Which statement is true?
    a. The dashed line represents how to lower the break-even on a common stock.
    b. The solid line shows that the break-even point is 35.
    c. The solid-line configuration is that of a bull spread.
    d. All bull spreads have profit graphs with this shape when the expiration dates are different for both calls.

26. A bull spread is a:
    a. horizontal spread
    b. vertical spread
    c. diagonal spread
    d. trapezoidal spread

Refer to the following graph for question 27.

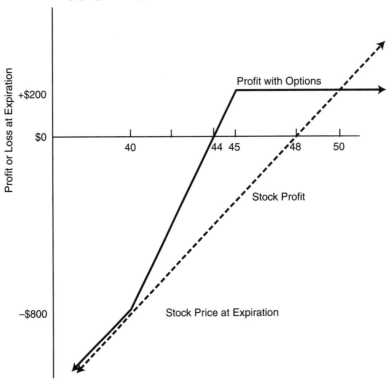

27. Which statement is true?
    a. The solid line represents a bull spread.
    b. This position has risk when the stock stabilizes anywhere above 50.
    c. The two strategies depicted – stock profit and profit with options – are equally profitable anywhere above 45.
    d. The break-even point is lowered from 48 to 44.

28. When you buy a call at one striking price and sell another call at a lower striking price, you create a:
    a. Put bear spread.
    b. Call bear spread.
    c. Ratio call write.
    d. Delta spread.

29. When set up with call options, a bear spread is a:
  a. debit transaction
  b. neutral transaction
  c. credit transaction
  d. profitable transaction

Refer to the following graph for question 30.

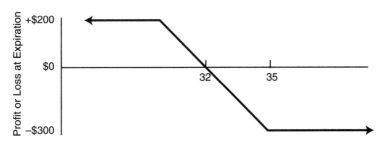

Stock Price at Expiration

30. Which statement is **NOT** true?
  a. The position becomes profitable when the stock moves below 32.
  b. The break-even point is 32.
  c. The configuration is that of a bear spread.
  d. None of the above.

31. The maximum risk in a call bear spread equals:
  a. Difference in striking prices – credit received + commissions.
  b. Collateral investment required.
  c. Net credit received.
  d. Both a and b.

32. The basic option strategy is to sell _____ _____ and buy _____ _____.
  a. Intrinisic value – time value
  b. Time value – intrinsic value
  c. Call options – put options.
  d. Put options – call options.

33. A bear spread is a:
   a. vertical spread
   b. horizontal spread
   c. diagonal spread
   d. trapezoidal spread

34. To establish a calendar spread:
   a. sell a near-term call and buy an intermediate-term call
   b. sell a near-term call and buy a long-term call
   c. sell an intermediate-term call and buy a long-term call
   d. any of the above

Refer to the following graph for question 35.

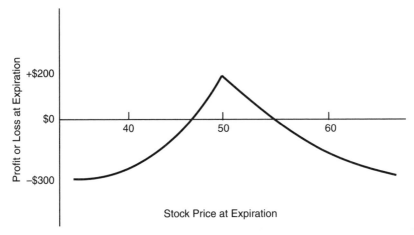

35. Which statement is true?
   a. The spread is profitable between 46 and 55.
   b. The maximum possible loss is $300.
   c. At 40 or 60, there is some time premium left.
   d. All of the above.

36. A calendar spread is a:
   a. horizontal spread
   b. vertical spread
   c. diagonal spread
   d. none of the above

37. As volatility increases, a calendar spread _____; as volatility decreases, the spread _____.
   a. Shrinks – widens
   b. Shrinks – shrinks
   c. Widens – shrinks
   d. Widens – widens

38. In a calendar spread, the easiest and most conservative type of downside defensive action is to:
   a. Roll down.
   b. Sell and buy more options.
   c. Close the position.
   d. Do nothing.

39. In a butterfly spread, which statement is **NOT** true?
   a. 3 striking prices are involved.
   b. 4 commissions are needed.
   c. The position has limited risk.
   d. The margin required is 20% of the call price.

40. To establish a butterfly spread, you:
   a. Combine a bull spread and a bear spread.
   b. Buy calls and sell puts.
   c. Can expect no upside limit on profit.
   d. Subject yourself to unlimited risk.

Refer to the following graph for question 41.

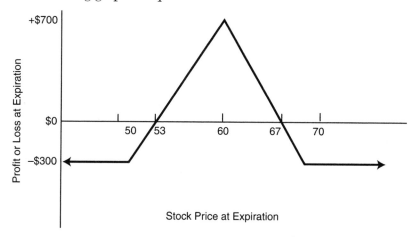

41. In this graph:
   a. The spread is profitable between 53 and 67.
   b. The maximum possible loss is theoretically infinite.
   c. The maximum profit is at 67.
   d. None of the above.

42. In a ratio call spread, the greatest risk occurs when the stock price:
   a. rises
   b. falls
   c. stays the same
   d. either a or b

Refer to the following graph for question 43.

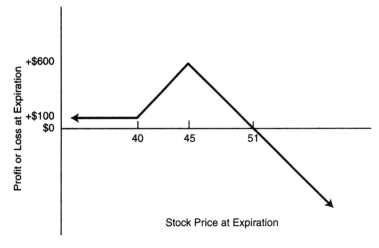

43. Which statement is true?
   a. The maximum potential profit is $100.
   b. The maximum potential profit occurs at 45.
   c. The break-even point is at 40.
   d. The maximum potential loss is $100.

44. A ratio spread is:
   a. bullish
   b. neutral
   c. bearish
   d. riskless

45. To determine the correct ratio to use in a delta neutral spread, divide the
_____ by the _____.
    a. Delta of the written call – the delta of the purchased call.
    b. Delta of the purchased call – delta of the written call.
    c. Delta of the purchased call – striking price of the written call.
    d. Delta of the written call – striking price of the purchased call.

46. If a ratio call spread is established for a credit, what can be said?
    a. The position cannot lose money if the stock remains below the higher striking price.
    b. There is limited risk in the spread.
    c. The maximum profit potential is equal to the credit received.
    d. Both a and c are true.

47. To establish a ratio calendar spread, a trader:
    a. Buys near-term calls and sells a larger number of intermediate- or long-term calls.
    b. Buys near-term calls and sells a smaller number of intermediate- or long-term calls.
    c. Sells near-term calls and buys a larger number of intermediate- or long-term calls.
    d. Sells near-term calls and buys a smaller number of intermediate- or long-term calls.

48. A ratio calendar spread should be closed if the stock price:
    a. Breaks out above technical resistance.
    b. Breaks out below a support level.
    c. Breaks out above the eventual break-even point at expiration.
    d. Both a and b.

49. When a ratio call calendar spread is established using out-of-the-money calls, what can be said?
    a. The stock price must fall for the spread to profit.
    b. There is limited risk in the position.
    c. A large profit could eventually accrue if the written calls first expire worthless.
    d. There is unlimited profit potential immediately.

50. Margin calls are possible on a ratio calendar spread because the naked calls are:
   a. uncovered.
   b. out-of-the-money.
   c. marked to the market.
   d. none of the above.

Refer to the following graph for question 51.

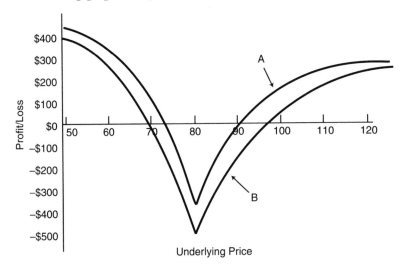

51. Which statement is **NOT** true?
   a. The graph reflects a reverse calendar spread.
   b. The spread is not profitable if the stock is equal to the striking price.
   c. The spread becomes profitable if the stock price rises above 98.
   d. The spread is profitable at any price between 70 and 98.

52. In a backspread, you sell a call at one striking price and buy several calls at:
   a. A higher striking price.
   b. A lower striking price.
   c. The same striking price.
   d. Various striking prices.

53. To establish a reverse calendar spread, a trader:
   a. Sells a short-term call option and buys a higher-priced call option.
   b. Sells a long-term call option and buys a lower-priced call option.
   c. Sells a short-term call option and buys a longer-term call option.
   d. Sells a long-term call option and buys a shorter-term call option.

54. The maximum loss at expiration for a reverse ratio spread occurs:
   a. at the striking price of the purchased call
   b. at the striking price of the sold call
   c. below the striking price of the purchased call
   d. below the striking price of the sold call

55. Which statement is **NOT** true?
   a. A reverse ratio call spread is also termed a call backspread.
   b. There are net long calls in a reverse ratio call spread.
   c. A reverse ratio call spread has unlimited risk.
   d. A reverse ratio call spread is normally established for a credit.

56. In a diagonal bear spread, you would:
   a. Sell a call with a lower striking price and nearer expiration, buy a call with a higher striking price and farther out expiration date.
   b. Buy a longer-term call at a lower striking price, sell a near-term call at a higher striking price.
   c. Have different striking prices, but the same expiration date.
   d. Buy more than one longer-term call against the short-term call sold.

57. In a diagonal bull spread, you would:
   a. Sell a call with a lower striking price and nearer expiration, buy a call with a higher striking price and farther out expiration date.
   b. Buy a longer-term call at a lower striking price, sell a near-term call at a higher striking price.
   c. Have the same striking price, but different expiration dates.
   d. Buy more than one longer-term call against the short-term call sold.

58. A diagonal spread involves:
   a. different striking prices and the same expiration date
   b. same striking prices and different expiration dates
   c. different striking price and different expiration dates
   d. different stock prices and different expiration dates

59. In a diagonal spread, the maximum profit at expiration occurs when the stock is:
   a. near the striking price of the written call
   b. near the striking price of the purchased call
   c. above the striking price of the written call
   d. above the striking price of the purchased call

60. As the price of the underlying stock declines, a put:
   a. Decreases in value.
   b. Increases in value.
   c. Maintains its original value.
   d. Expires.

Refer to the following graph for question 61.

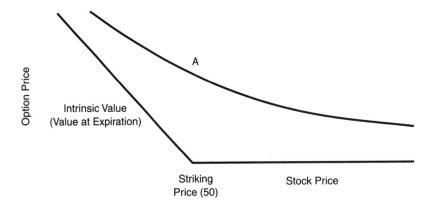

61. Which statement is true?
   a. The graph shows the configuration of a put option price curve.
   b. Curve A reflects the decline in intrinsic value as the option nears expiration.
   c. The intrinsic value line reflects a loss in value as the stock falls below the striking price.
   d. None of the above.

62. As the ex-dividend date of a stock nears, the time value premium of in-the-money puts on the stock will:
   a. Remain unaffected.
   b. Equal or exceed the dividend payment.
   c. Decline by the amount of the dividend payment.
   d. Behave in the same way as for a call option.

63. The put writer who is assigned must:
  a. Receive stock.
  b. Sell stock.
  c. Sell the option.
  d. Buy an offsetting call.

64. The exercise of a put results in:
  a. Selling stock at the current market price.
  b. Buying stock at the current market price.
  c. Selling stock at the striking price.
  d. Buying stock at the striking price.

65. An in-the-money put option:
  a. Loses its time value premium faster than a call option.
  b. Gains in time value premium faster than a call option.
  c. Gains and loses its time value premium in the same way as a call option.
  d. None of the above.

66. A put purchase is used for speculative purposes when:
  a. You expect a decline in the underlying stock's price.
  b. You expect a rise in the underlying stock's price.
  c. You have no opinion on the underlying stock's price.
  d. A put purchase is always speculative.

Refer to the following graph for question 67.

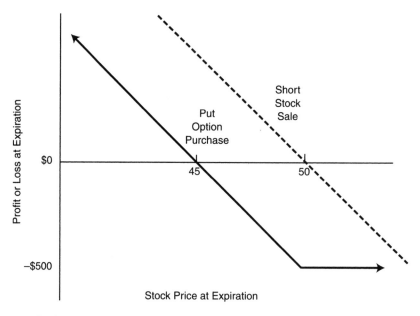

67. Which statement is true?
    a. Both strategies involve unlimited risk.
    b. Both strategies involve limited risk.
    c. The put option purchase obligates the holder to pay dividends on the underlying stock.
    d. The put option purchase involves more limited risk than the short sale.

68. A put option purchase is an alternative to:
    a. A short sale of stock.
    b. Writing covered calls.
    c. Rolling down.
    d. Exercising a call.

Refer to the following graph for question 69.

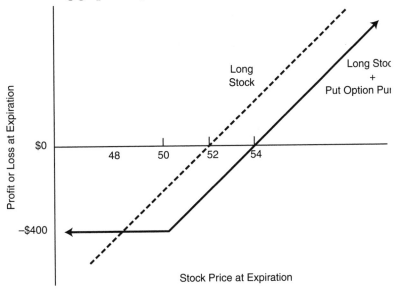

69. Which statement is **NOT** true?
  a. The graph represents a put option purchase compared to a long position in the underlying stock.
  b. The maximum risk of the solid line is $400.
  c. A put option purchase limits the risk of owning stock.
  d. Stock protected by a put option behaves just like the ownership of a call option.

70. The purchase of stock coupled with the purchase of a put *and* the sale of a call is called:
  a. Protective collar.
  b. Bull spread.
  c. Call purchase.
  d. Bear spread.

71. Put purchases can be used:
  a. to limit upside risk on a stock that is shorted
  b. to limit downside loss on a stock that is shorted
  c. to maximize upside profit on a stock that is owned
  d. to limit downside loss on a stock that is owned

72. To eliminate the risk of large losses on a covered write, you may purchase:
  a. an in-the-money put
  b. an at-the-money put
  c. an out-of-the-money put
  d. an out-of-the-money call

73. To create a straddle, you would purchase a put and a call with:
  a. same underlying stock, different striking prices, and same expiration date
  b. same underlying stock, same striking price, and same expiration date
  c. different underlying stocks, same striking price, and same expiration date
  d. same underlying stock, same striking price, and different expiration dates

Refer to the following graph for question 74.

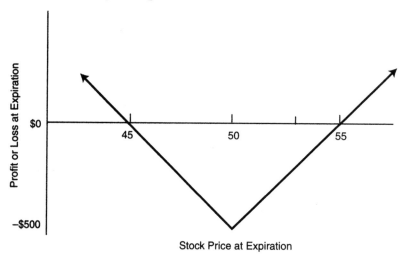

74. The graph represents:
  a. A strangle purchase.
  b. A straddle purchase.
  c. A reverse hedge with puts.
  d. A trade against the straddle.

75. In a straddle, the probability of losing your entire investment:
- **a.** Is great.
- **b.** Is moderate.
- **c.** Is small.
- **d.** Cannot be determined.

76. A strangle purchase involves buying a put and a call with:
- **a.** same expiration date, different striking prices
- **b.** same expiration date, same striking price
- **c.** different expiration dates, different striking prices
- **d.** different expiration dates, same striking price

Refer to the following graph for question 77.

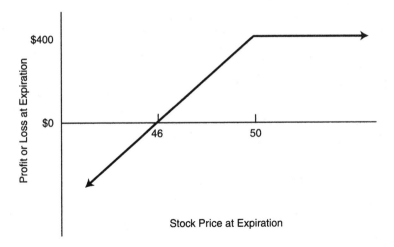

77. Which statement is **NOT** true?
- **a.** The maximum profit is $400 and the potential profit levels off at 50.
- **b.** The configuration is that of an uncovered put sale.
- **c.** The downside loss is limited only by the fact that the underlying stock cannot go below zero.
- **d.** None of the above.

78. In both an uncovered put strategy and a covered call strategy, the probability of achieving the maximum profit is greater if the position is established with the stock:
    a. Above the striking price.
    b. Below the striking price.
    c. At the striking price.
    d. Either above or below the striking price.

79. A ratio put write achieves its maximum profit:
    a. at the striking price of the underlying stock.
    b. above the striking price of the underlying stock.
    c. below the striking price of the written options.
    d. at the striking price of the written options.

80. To establish a naked put sale, you would:
    a. Sell a put, short the underlying stock.
    b. Sell a put, do not short underlying stock.
    c. Buy a put, short the underlying stock.
    d. Buy a put, do not short underlying stock.

81. In a covered straddle write, you would:
    a. Sell an out-of-the-money call, sell an out-of-the-money put, and buy the stock.
    b. Sell the straddle without owning the underlying stock.
    c. Buy the straddle and sell the stock short.
    d. Own the underlying stock and simultaneously write a straddle.

82. The maximum profit on a covered straddle write is the:
    a. Straddle premium minus striking price plus initial stock price.
    b. Straddle premium plus striking price minus initial stock price.
    c. Time value premium minus striking price plus initial stock price.
    d. Time value premium plus striking price minus initial stock price.

83. To establish a strangle write, an investor could:
    a. Sell an out-of-the-money call and sell an out-of-the-money put.
    b. Sell an in-the-money put and an in-the-money call.
    c. Sell an in-the-money put and an out-of-the-money call.
    d. Do any of the above.

84. Compared to a straddle writer, the strangle writer's potential profit range:
    a. Is wider.
    b. Is narrower.
    c. Is about the same.
    d. Cannot be determined.

85. To create a synthetic short sale of stock, you would:
    a. Buy a call, sell a put with the same terms.
    b. Buy a put, sell a call, where the striking price of the put is lower than that of the call.
    c. Buy a put, sell a call, where the striking price of the call is lower than that of the put.
    d. Buy a put, sell a call with the same terms.

Refer to the following graph for question 86.

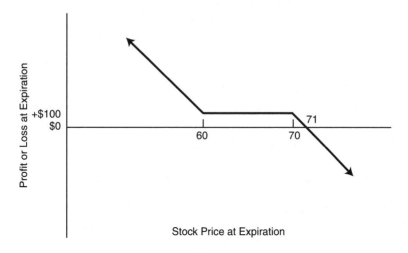

86. In the graph:
    a. If the underlying rises substantially by expiration, large profits are possible.
    b. If the stock drops well below 70, unlimited losses are possible.
    c. If the underlying remains between 60 and 70 at expiration, the profit is limited.
    d. This is a bullish strategy.

87. Compared to stock ownership, a synthetic long position requires:
   a. A much smaller investment.
   b. A much greater investment.
   c. About the same investment.
   d. None of the above.

88. A bearish position can be established by which method?
   a. Buy a put at one striking price and sell a call at a higher striking price.
   b. Buy a put at one striking price and sell a put at a higher striking price.
   c. Buy a call at one striking price and sell a put at a higher striking price.
   d. Both a and c.

89. To establish a put bear spread, you would:
   a. Sell a put at a higher strike and buy a put at a lower strike.
   b. Sell a put at a lower strike and buy a put at a higher strike.
   c. Sell a put with a longer expiration date and buy a put with a shorter expiration date.
   d. Sell a put with a shorter expiration date and buy a put with a longer expiration date.

90. The maximum profit in a put bull spread occurs when the underlying stock:
   a. Declines.
   b. Rises.
   c. Remains within a certain range.
   d. There is no maximum profit in a put bull spread.

91. To establish a put calendar spread, the investor should:
   a. Sell a near-term put and buy a longer-term put, both with the same strike price.
   b. Buy a near-term put and sell a longer-term put, both with the same strike price.
   c. Sell a near-term put and buy a longer-term put, with different strike prices.
   d. Buy a near-term put and sell a longer-term put, with different strike prices.

92. What are the characteristics of a butterfly spread?
    a. High risk, limited profit
    b. Limited risk, high profit
    c. Limited risk, limited profit
    d. High risk, high profit

93. A calendar combination is typically made up of:
    a. An out-of-the-money call calendar spread and an out-of-the-money put calendar spread
    b. An in-the-money call calendar spread and an in-the-money put calendar spread
    c. An out-of-the-money call calendar spread and an in-the-money put calendar spread
    d. An out-of-the-money put calendar spread and an in-the-money call calendar spread

94. For the best chance (highest probability) of capturing the entire near-term premium, you would create a:
    a. Calendar combination.
    b. Calendar straddle.
    c. Diagonal butterfly.
    d. Protected straddle write.

Refer to the following graph for question 95.

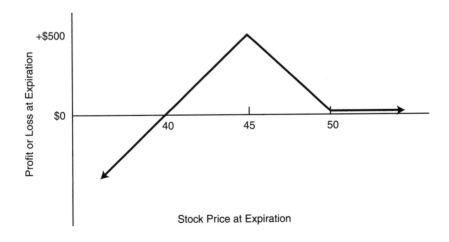

95. Which statement is **NOT** true?
   a. The profitable range is between 40 and infinity.
   b. The graph reflects a ratio put spread.
   c. Losses can be large.
   d. The maximum profit is realized if the underlying stock is at 50 at expiration.

96. To establish a ratio put calendar spread:
   a. Buy a longer-term put and sell a larger quantity of shorter-term puts, all with the same striking price.
   b. Buy puts at one striking price and sell more puts at a lower striking price.
   c. Buy puts at one striking price and sell more puts at a higher striking price.
   d. Buy a short-term put and sell a larger quantity of longer-term puts, all with the same striking price.

97. The downside break-even price of a ratio put spread is:
   a. higher strike price minus maximum profit potential divided by number of naked puts.
   b. lower strike price minus maximum profit potential divided by number of naked puts.
   c. lower strike price minus maximum profit potential divided by number of short puts.
   d. strike price differential minus maximum profit potential divided by number of naked puts.

Refer to the following graph for question 98.

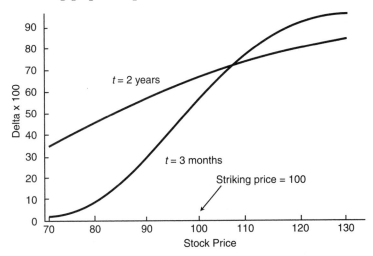

98. The graph compares the deltas of two calls. Which statement is true?
    a. The delta of the at-the-money LEAPS is small.
    b. The deltas of the 3-month call and the 2-year LEAPS call are about equal when the options are approximately 5% in-the-money.
    c. The delta of the 2-year LEAPS changes more dramatically when the stock moves than does the delta of the 3-month option.
    d. None of the above.

99. Which specification does **NOT** apply to LEAPS?
    a. Type (put or call).
    b. Underlying stock name (or symbol).
    c. Expiration date.
    d. Price of underlying stock.

100. LEAPS differ from regular equity options in that:
    a. They are longer-term.
    b. They expire on the Saturday following the third Friday of the expiration month.
    c. There is no standardized striking price interval.
    d. Both a and c.

Final Examination Answers

1.	c	26.	b	51.	d	76.	a
2.	a	27.	d	52.	a	77.	d
3.	d	28.	b	53.	d	78.	a
4.	d	29.	c	54.	a	79.	d
5.	b	30.	d	55.	c	80.	b
6.	c	31.	d	56.	a	81.	d
7.	d	32.	b	57.	b	82.	b
8.	c	33.	a	58.	c	83.	d
9.	b	34.	d	59.	a	84.	a
10.	c	35.	d	60.	b	85.	d
11.	d	36.	a	61.	a	86.	c
12.	c	37.	c	62.	b	87.	a
13.	d	38.	d	63.	a	88.	a
14.	b	39.	d	64.	c	89.	b
15.	c	40.	a	65.	a	90.	b
16.	b	41.	a	66.	a	91.	a
17.	c	42.	a	67.	d	92.	c
18.	d	43.	b	68.	a	93.	a
19.	b	44.	b	69.	a	94.	a
20.	d	45.	b	70.	a	95.	d
21.	b	46.	a	71.	d	96.	a
22.	a	47.	d	72.	c	97.	b
23.	d	48.	c	73.	b	98.	b
24.	b	49.	c	74.	b	99.	d
25.	c	50.	c	75.	c	100.	d

NOTES

NOTES

NOTES

NOTES

NOTES

NOTES

NOTES